THE TRAGEDY OF
King Lear

EDITED BY
George Lyman Kittredge

Revised by Irving Ribner

William Shakespeare

THE TRAGEDY OF

King Lear

XEROX COLLEGE PUBLISHING
LEXINGTON, MASSACHUSETTS • TORONTO

PREFACE

The New Kittredge Shakespeares

The publication of George Lyman Kittredge's *Complete Works of Shakespeare* in 1936 was a landmark in Shakespeare scholarship. The teacher who for almost half a century had dominated and shaped the direction of Shakespearean study in America produced what was recognized widely as the finest edition of Shakespeare up to his time. In the preface to this edition Kittredge indicated his editorial principles; these allowed a paramount authority to the Folio of 1623 and countenanced few departures from it while, at the same time, refusing to "canonize the heedless type-setters of the Elizabethan printing house." Kittredge's work was marked by a judicious conservatism and a common sense rarely found in equal measure in earlier editors of Shakespeare. In the thirty-odd years which have gone by since the appearance of this monumental volume, however, considerable advances have been made in the establishment of Shakespeare's text, and our body of knowledge about the dates, sources, and general historical background of Shakespeare's plays has vastly increased. The present revision is designed to apply this new knowledge to Kittredge's work so that it may have as much value to the student and general reader of today as it had to those of thirty years ago.

Before his death Kittredge had issued, in addition to *The Complete Works,* separate editions of sixteen of the plays, each copiously annotated. Some of the notes were unusually elaborate, but they interpreted Shakespeare's language with a fullness and precision attained by few other commentators, for Kittredge had few equals in his intimate knowledge of Elizabethan English. In freshly annotating the plays I have, accordingly, tried to use

Kittredge's own notes as fully as space would permit. Where I have repeated his distinctive language or recorded his characteristic critical opinions, I have followed the note with the symbol [κ]; where Kittredge's definition of a term can be found in essentially the same words in other editions, I have not used the identifying symbol. Every annotator draws upon the full body of the notes of earlier editors, and to give credit for every note is impossible. Notes have been placed at page bottoms.

The brief introductions which Kittredge wrote for the plays have been replaced by new ones, for what seemed like indisputable fact some thirty years ago often appears today to be much more uncertain, and many new issues of which Kittredge was not aware have been raised in recent criticism. The new introductions seek to present what are now generally agreed to be basic facts about the plays and to give some indications of the directions which modern criticism has taken, although specific analyses of individual plays are avoided.

Such great authority attaches to Kittredge's text that it has not frequently — and never lightly — been departed from. Where changes have been made, they have usually involved the restoration of copy-text readings now generally accepted in place of the emendations of eighteenth- and nineteenth-century editors of which Kittredge, in spite of his extraordinary conservatism in this regard, sometimes too easily approved. Only rarely has an emendation been adopted in the present revision which was not also adopted by Kittredge. All departures from the copy-texts are indicated in the notes, emendations followed by the names of the editors by whom they were first proposed. Wherever Kittredge's text has been departed from for any reason, his reading is given in the notes. Modern spelling has in a few instances been substituted for Elizabethan forms which are mere spelling variations but which Kittredge nevertheless retained. His punctuation has not been altered except in a few very rare instances.

The system of recording elisions and contractions which Kittredge explained in his introduction to *The Complete Works* has been retained, as has his method of preserving to the fullest the copy-text stage directions, with all additions to them enclosed within square brackets. Although modern editors recognize the vagueness of the place settings of Elizabethan plays and are reluctant to include the place designations so favoured by eighteenth- and nineteenth-century editors, much historical interest nevertheless attaches to these, and Kittredge's place designations accordingly have been retained between square brackets. Kittredge's attempt to retain the line numbering of the Globe text, which resulted in considerable irregularity in prose passages, has been abandoned, and the lines of each play have been freshly numbered. Kittredge's act and scene divisions have been retained, as has his practice of surrounding by square brackets those divisions which are not in the copy-texts.

The *New Kittredge Shakespeares* include individual editions of each of the plays, the sonnets, and the minor poems, and a new edition of *The Complete Works* in a single volume. A comprehensive introduction to Shakespeare's life, times, and theatrical milieu is available both as a separate volume and as an introduction to *The Complete Works*.

IRVING RIBNER

INTRODUCTION

The Tragedy of King Lear

◇◇◇◇◇
◇◇◇◇◇ On St. Stephen's Night, December 26, 1606, Shake-
◇◇◇◇◇ speare's company performed *King Lear* before King
James I and his court at Whitehall. This fact was recorded in
the Stationers' Register when the play was entered there on
November 26, 1607, and it appears duly upon the title page of
the quarto edition (Q¹) printed for Nathaniel Butter in 1608,
"to be sold at his shop in Pauls Church-yard at the signe of the
Pide Bull neere St. Austins Gate." That the Whitehall perform-
ance was the play's first is unlikely. There is, in fact, some reason
to believe that the play was being publicly staged in late 1604
or early 1605. On May 8, 1605, there was entered in the Stationers' Register an old play, *The True Chronicle History of
King Leir,* written sometime before 1594. When this work was
printed in 1605 its title page claimed it to have been "diuers
and sundry times lately acted." That so old a play should have
been frequently acted as late as 1605 seems very unlikely; the
publisher's claim suggests rather that he was trying to pass off
this old piece as Shakespeare's play, and if this is true Shakespeare's *King Lear* must by 1605 have been staged sufficiently
often to have been well known to the public. The old play —
which has often been attributed to George Peele, but carries no
author's name on its title page — was in fact one of Shakespeare's
principal sources for *King Lear.* There is no reason to assume,
however, that he began to think about the subject only after the
appearance of this play in 1605. Although the play's theatre
history is obscure, it is more than likely that Shakespeare had
had ample opportunity to become familiar with it before its
publication. For all we know, he may himself have acted in it.

The likeliest supposition, however, is that the prompt-book of this old *Leir* play had at some early date passed into the possession of Shakespeare's company, for it seems clear that he had close access to it while writing his own *King Lear*. Edgar's mad talk, and particularly the names of the devils he mentions, resemble very closely Samuel Harsnet's account of cases of supposed demoniacal possession in *A Declaration of Egregious Popish Impostures*, published in 1603.

THE TEXTUAL PROBLEM

There are actually two quartos of *King Lear* which bear the date of 1608. The first is that printed by Nathaniel Butter and usually called the "Pied Bull quarto" because of its title-page statement. The second (Q^2) was actually printed by William Jaggard in 1619 with a false title page and was based upon Q^1 of 1608. Q^1 was a very carelessly printed quarto, partially corrected during the course of printing, so that the twelve extant copies which have come down to us exhibit a large number of variant readings. Both corrected and uncorrected sheets seem to have been haphazardly bound together. It seems, moreover, to have been some kind of derivative text. Earlier scholars thought that it may have been derived by stenography, but this is hardly likely, and the very notion that texts could be pirated in that manner has come into much scholarly disfavour. Others have suggested that it was derived by memorial reconstruction, either by a single reporter who had closely studied the prompt-book, by a whole company of actors working together to prepare a prompt-book to replace one lost or unavailable to them, or — as has been most recently suggested — by the two boys who played the parts of Goneril and Regan, the one reading from Shakespeare's foul papers while the other wrote down what was being dictated, but each depending at times upon his own memory. There is no end to the possibilities, and others no doubt will continue to be suggested. Although Q^1 does not have the usual marks of a "bad quarto" it obviously does not present a reliable text of the play that Shakespeare wrote. Its exact nature and origins remain a puzzle.

In the folio of 1623 (F^1) appeared a text of the play considerably shorter than that of Q^1, omitting some three hundred lines, but at the same time supplying about one hundred lines not in Q^1 and correcting a good many of Q^1's errors while retaining others. The relation of these various texts to one another has been a matter of considerable scholarly debate. It used to be believed that F^1 was set entirely from a copy of Q^1 which had been corrected carefully by reference to an authoritative playhouse manuscript. While most of the play was probably set in this manner, some use must have been made of Q^2 as well, and it has been suggested that the printer had in his possession a corrected copy of this quarto as well as of Q^1. There also is a likelihood that some parts of F^1 were set directly from manuscript without reference to either quarto.

Probably we shall never know the entire truth. It is clear, however, that F^1 must serve as our basic text for *King Lear*, and that we must make free use of Q^1 wherever F^1 is deficient. This is the procedure which has been followed in the present edition. All departures from F^1 are recorded in the notes. Q^1 variants of F^1 readings are listed in the notes only when they are of special interest or have been the subject of scholarly dispute. A third quarto, printed in 1655, has no independent authority.

The F^1 text contains full act and scene division, which is followed here with one deviation: the Globe text is followed in the division of the F^1 Act II, Scene II into Scenes II, III, and IV. Although it is likely that the action was, in fact, continuous at these points and the departure from F^1 quite unnecessary, these divisions have become conventional in editions of *King Lear*, and they are preserved here for their historical interest.

It is obvious that in dealing with a play whose textual history is so complex and uncertain as that of *King Lear*, an editor must exercise a high degree of independent judgment; eclecticism simply cannot be avoided. Every variant between Q^1 and F^1 must be considered on its own merits, and even where both texts agree it is possible that F^1 is merely preserving a Q^1 reporter's error. Where variants appear to be of equal value in all respects, we may follow the principle that the F^1 reading must be preferred to that of Q^1, no matter what our own literary tastes or preferences may be, but the very judgment that two variant readings are of equal value ultimately depends upon the editor's own predilections.

THE LEAR STORY

The core of the *Lear* story is an old folk tale which has its analogues throughout the folk literature of Western Europe, one of the best known being that of Cinderella. Lear (Llyr, Ler) himself was a shadowy figure of ancient Celtic mythology about whose children stories circulated in Irish and Welsh. Geoffrey of Monmouth, Bishop of St. Asaph, in his *Historia Regum Britanniae,* written toward the close of the twelfth century, seems to have been the first to associate the folk tale with Lear and to place him in the line of kings descended from the Trojan Brute, grandson of Æneas and supposed founder of Britain. While purporting to be telling the history of his country, Geoffrey gathered together the romantic folk literature of his age. The line of British kings whose stories he recounted, beginning with Brute, including such figures as Locrine, Gorboduc, Lear, and Cymbeline and ending with King Arthur, became regular features of later chronicles of England. The story of Lear appears in a great many places, including among those with which we may be certain that Shakespeare was familiar, Edmund Spenser's *Faerie Queene* (Book II, Canto 10), *A Mirror for Magistrates,* and Raphael Holinshed's *Chronicles of England, Scotland and Ireland,* which in the 1587 edition served as the principal source of all Shakespeare's plays on English history.

The historicity of the legend of Brute and his descendants, of which the *Lear* story was a part, was a matter of considerable dispute in Shakespeare's England. The Tudor kings had based their claim to the throne in part upon their supposed descent from King Arthur, and they did not encourage attacks upon the notion of Arthur's existence. Although respected antiquarians such as John Leland and John Caius had defended the authenticity of Geoffrey's pseudo history against such skeptics as Polydore Vergil, and although we do not know to what extent the skepticism of the scholars may have affected dramatists and their audiences, it is nevertheless true that Geoffrey's matter was so far removed from Shakespeare's contemporaries and so inherently folkloristic in nature, that it could never be regarded in precisely the same manner that actual history was regarded, and dramatists like Shakespeare who handled this matter felt less of a need for fidelity to their sources than they apparently felt when dealing with such figures as King John or Richard II. It still had about it the dignity of historical matter duly reported in the chronicles, and it could be treated as history was generally treated.

SHAKESPEARE'S SOURCES

That Shakespeare used Holinshed's version of the story is certain; he took from it various details, including the ducal titles of Cornwall and Albany. From Spenser's *Faerie Queene* he took his particular form of Cordelia's name and the detail of her death by hanging. In Holinshed and in *A Mirror for Magistrates,* from which he took various other details, Cordelia stabs herself in despair some seven years after the death of her father, whom she has succeeded as queen, when she has been taken prisoner by two nephews who have rebelled against rule by a woman. Shakespeare may also have known the accounts in Gerald Legh's *Accidence of Armoury* and William Warner's *Albion's England,* although it is impossible to establish specific indebtedness in these instances. He seems to have relied most heavily, however, upon the old play *The True Chronicle History of King Leir,* which includes only part of the story of Lear and his daughters as contained in the other versions.

Holinshed tells a double story. The major part of his account deals with Lear's relations with his daughters, ending with his joyful reconciliation with Cordelia and his restoration to his throne and two years of further rule, after which he dies a natural death. Holinshed concludes his account with the further story of Cordelia, who succeeded her father and ruled for five years before her nephews, the sons of Goneril and Regan, rose against her, captured her, and caused her to commit suicide. The old *Leir* play tells the story up to Lear's restoration to his throne.

It is a sentimental fairy tale with never a hint that Leir is anything but a virtuous old man who has made the one foolish
mistake of disinheriting his daughter. He survives all of his consequent hardships through his faith in divine providence, and in
the fairy tale tradition, sorrow gives way to joy and reconciliation, vice is punished, and virtue is rewarded.

SIDNEY'S ARCADIA

Shakespeare made a single tragic story out of the two episodes in
Holinshed by eliminating the interval of seven years and by
identifying the rebellion against Cordelia by her nephews with
the war waged by Cordelia and the King of France against her
sisters and their husbands on behalf of her father. Shakespeare
gave a further tragic cast to the story by fusing it with a subplot
from a quite alien source. The story of Gloucester and his sons
he took from an episode in *The Arcadia,* a lengthy prose pas-
toral romance by Sir Philip Sidney, first published in 1590. In
the tenth chapter of the second book occurs the story of the blind
King of Paphlagonia and his two sons, whom he transformed
into Gloucester, Edgar, and Edmund. It has been suggested that
Shakespeare may have adapted the Lear story in terms of certain
suggestions which he found in Sidney's story. Certainly he shaped
his two plots as close parallels to one another. The initial folly
of Lear is echoed by that of Gloucester, and both men must
undergo a similar tragic progression, the mental anguish of Lear
being paralleled by the physical sufferings of Gloucester. Just as
Lear was truly mad when the world thought him sane and ac-
quired true wisdom only during his ordeal of madness on the
heath, Gloucester was in fact blind while he had his eyes and
learned to see truly only when they were put out by his unnatural son. By means of the parallel tragedy of Gloucester
Shakespeare gave a range to his tragedy such as he was able to
achieve in no other play. The double action shows us the tragedy
of a king and the tragedy of his subject; as the tragedy of
Gloucester parallels that of Lear it lends to both a sense of
universal validity.

In Sidney's *Arcadia* Shakespeare may have found the theme of royal responsibility which he made so much a part of his play, although it is not an issue at all in the old *King Leir*. Sidney's romance, both in its main plot of King Basilius and his daughters and in the subplot of the King of Paphlagonia and his sons which Shakespeare borrowed, is concerned with what happens to a kingdom when its ruler abandons to another person the obligation to rule his people until God relieves him of this responsibility by death — a cornerstone of the Tudor conception of kingship.

RENAISSANCE NATURALISM

In Gloucester's bastard son, Edmund, Shakespeare gave his play a kind of villain who has no parallel in other versions of the *Lear* story, one whose action represents a philosophical position which Shakespeare's play subjects to close analysis. Edmund stands for a new skepticism which in the Jacobean era was challenging the settled values inherited from an earlier time, and which came to be known as naturalism. For Edmund nature, the goddess whom he serves and by whose laws he seeks to live, is entirely mechanistic. It is the ultimate power in the universe, governed by fixed laws of cause and effect, entirely independent of any supernatural influence. Human reason is the power to understand the laws of nature and thus, to at least some degree, to control them, and it is only this power of reason which sets man apart from the lower animals who are equally subject to nature's laws. To the orthodox Christian, of course, nature could never be conceived of as other than the creation of God, governed by God's law, and human reason, if not perverted, could lead man only to an acceptance of God's law.

Edmund's primary drive is for power, and his "reason" is the ability to manipulate nature and other men for his own advantage. It is fitting that he should be a bastard, for, conceived outside of God's harmonious order with its moral standards, he can deny all of those benevolent human feelings which are a part of that order, proceeding from the love of God for man. These include loyalty, the bonds of family, and the system of primogeniture, which to Shakespeare's contemporaries insured the orderly movement of the world's affairs from generation to generation. For Edmund there is nothing in man that is not a part of his mechanistic nature, and thus his own being is a law unto itself which can recognize no externally imposed system of morality. But Shakespeare allows him at the end to see the shallowness of all in which he has believed, and as his final act he attempts to save Cordelia, to perform one virtuous deed without possible gain for himself.

REGENERATION OR DESPAIR

Edmund's view of the world is a brutal and horrifying one. In his final defeat by his brother Edgar, who is conventional — and to many readers less attractive — in his affirmation of traditional Christian patience, there is some indication that Edmund's brand of naturalism does not represent Shakespeare's own philosophical position in the play. Critics have been strongly divided about Shakespeare's view of the world in *King Lear*. To some Lear's sufferings mirror only the meaningless torture of mankind in a world in which human goodness is incapable of expressing itself in action and in which man is never more than the suffering pawn of brute forces beyond his comprehension. This view has in recent times been perhaps best expressed by D. G. James in *The Dream of Learning* (Oxford: The Clarendon Press, 1951).

Still other critics have regarded the sufferings of Lear and Gloucester not as meaningless and futile but as a purgative process through which each acquires a knowledge of himself and of his world which he had never had before and thus experiences a regeneration of spirit at the price of pain. The play is thus seen as one which, rather than offer us a vision of total despair, allows us to participate imaginatively in a vision of human growth and regeneration. Good and evil in this play are pitted against one another clearly and surely. The good suffer and die, but evil, although it destroys the good, works itself out, leaving such characters as Albany and Edgar alive to begin new life upon the ruins of the old. The surest fact about evil which emerges from the world of *King Lear* is that it is a force contrary to nature, an aberration in the social order and in the human being, and that ultimately it must destroy itself. The greatest and most important value in this play is that of enduring and self-sacrificing love, and if King Lear does indeed undergo a spiritual regeneration before his death, it is through his recognition at last of this supreme value in his child Cordelia.

The Tragedy of
King Lear

[DRAMATIS PERSONÆ.

LEAR, *King of Britain.*
KING OF FRANCE.
DUKE OF BURGUNDY.
DUKE OF CORNWALL.
DUKE OF ALBANY.
EARL OF KENT.
EARL OF GLOUCESTER.
EDGAR, *son to* GLOUCESTER.
EDMUND, *bastard son to* GLOUCESTER.
CURAN, *a courtier.*
Old Man, tenant to GLOUCESTER.
Doctor.
LEAR'S *Fool.*
OSWALD, *Steward to* GONERIL.
A Captain under EDMUND'S *command.*
Gentleman, attendant on CORDELIA.
A Herald.
Servants to CORNWALL.
GONERIL,
REGAN, } *daughters to* LEAR.
CORDELIA,
Knights attending on LEAR, *Officers, Messengers, Soldiers,*
Attendants.

SCENE. — *Britain.*]

Act One

◇◇◇

SCENE I. [King Lear's *Palace.*]

Enter Kent, Gloucester, *and* Edmund. [Kent *and* Gloucester *converse.* Edmund *stands back.*]

KENT. I thought the King had more affected the Duke of Albany than Cornwall.

GLOU. It did always seem so to us; but now, in the division of the kingdom, it appears not which of the Dukes he values most, for equalities are so weigh'd that curiosity 5 in neither can make choice of either's moiety.

KENT. Is not this your son, my lord?

GLOU. His breeding, sir, hath been at my charge. I have so often blush'd to acknowledge him that now I am braz'd to't. 10

KENT. I cannot conceive you.

GLOU. Sir, this young fellow's mother could; whereupon she grew round-womb'd, and had indeed, sir, a son for her cradle ere she had a husband for her bed. Do you smell a fault? 15

KENT. I cannot wish the fault undone, the issue of it being so proper.

I.I. 1 *more affected* been more inclined to favour [K]. 5–6 *equalities . . . moiety* the equality of their shares is so well balanced (so exact) that careful scrutiny on the part of neither can choose the other's share as better than his own [K]. *equalities* Q¹; F¹: "qualities." 8 *breeding* rearing, education. 9 *braz'd* hardened — literally, plated with brass [K]. 11 *conceive* understand. Gloucester puns on the word. 17 *proper* handsome.

1

GLOU.   But I have, sir, a son by order of law, some year elder
than this, who yet is no dearer in my account. Though
this knave came something saucily into the world before   20
he was sent for, yet was his mother fair, there was good
sport at his making, and the whoreson must be acknowl-
edged. — Do you know this noble gentleman, Edmund?

EDM.   [comes forward] No, my lord.

GLOU.   My Lord of Kent. Remember him hereafter as my hon-   25
ourable friend.

EDM.   My services to your lordship.

KENT.   I must love you, and sue to know you better.

EDM.   Sir, I shall study deserving.

GLOU.   He hath been been out nine years, and away he shall   30
again.   *Sound a sennet.*
The King is coming.

> *Enter one bearing a coronet; then*
> Lear; *then the* Dukes of Albany *and*
> Cornwall; *next,* Goneril, Regan, Cor-
> delia, *with* Followers.

LEAR.   Attend the lords of France and Burgundy, Gloucester.

GLOU.   I shall, my liege.   *Exeunt* [Gloucester *and* Edmund].

LEAR.   Meantime we shall express our darker purpose.   35
Give me the map there. Know we have divided
In three our kingdom; and 'tis our fast intent

---

18 *some year* about a year.   19 *account* estimation.   20 *knave* boy, fellow (not
used in any pejorative sense, but as a term of affection). *saucily* (a) with
impertinence (b) in a bawdy manner.   22 *whoreson* Although the word does
mean "bastard" and is perfectly applicable to Edmund in that sense, Gloucester
seems to be using it in the general sense of "rogue," a term of affectionate
abuse. There is some irony here.   27 *services* duty.   29 *study deserving* make
every effort to be worthy of your favour [K].   30 *out* away from home.   31 s.d.
sennet a series of notes on a trumpet.   35 *darker purpose* more secret intentions. He has not yet revealed exactly how he will divide his kingdom — giving
the largest share to the daughter who loves him most.   37 *three* three parts — not
necessarily equal ones. *fast intent* fixed purpose.   39–44 *while we . . . prevented
now* F¹; not in Q¹.   40 *crawl* That Lear's old age is not feeble (however he may
express himself) is clear from the whole of Act I. He still goes a-hunting (I.III. 7)
[K].   42 *constant will* fixed purpose. *publish* announce publicly.   43 *dowers*
Apparently Goneril and Regan have married only recently and their dowries have

To shake all cares and business from our age,
Conferring them on younger strengths while we
Unburden'd crawl toward death. Our son of Cornwall,   40
And you, our no less loving son of Albany,
We have this hour a constant will to publish
Our daughters' several dowers, that future strife
May be prevented now. The princes, France and Bur-
          gundy,
Great rivals in our youngest daughter's love,   45
Long in our court have made their amorous sojourn,
And here are to be answer'd. Tell me, my daughters
(Since now we will divest us both of rule,
Interest of territory, cares of state),
Which of you shall we say doth love us most?   50
That we our largest bounty may extend
Where nature doth with merit challenge. Goneril,
Our eldest-born, speak first.

GON.   Sir, I love you more than word can wield the matter;
Dearer than eyesight, space, and liberty;   55
Beyond what can be valued, rich or rare;
No less than life, with grace, health, beauty, honour;
As much as child e'er lov'd, or father found;
A love that makes breath poor, and speech unable.
Beyond all manner of so much I love you.   60

COR.   [*aside*] What shall Cordelia speak? Love, and be silent.

LEAR.   Of all these bounds, even from this line to this,

not yet been determined.   44 *prevented* forestalled; hindered in advance [K].
48–9 *Since now . . . of state* F¹; not in Q¹.   52 *Where nature . . . challenge* to
her whose merit, added to my natural affection, constitutes a claim to the most
generous gift [K] *with merit* in addition to merit.   54 *word* F¹; Q¹, K: "words."
wield the matter serve to express the fact [K].   55 *space, and liberty* "Space" expresses the idea of "freedom from confinement"; "liberty" adds the idea of "personal freedom in action" [K].   56 *what* whatever, anything that [K].   57 *grace*
favour.   58 *found* discovered in his child.   60 *Beyond . . . so much* beyond
every kind of comparison that can be imagined; not — beyond the comparisons
that I have just expressed. "Manner" is the emphatic word [K].   62 *these bounds*
Lear indicates the boundaries in the map. Though he seems to give Goneril and
Regan a chance to obtain the largest of the three shares, he has already determined
their portions (as we learn from lines 1–6), and he is reserving the "largest bounty"
for Cordelia, since he is confident that she loves him most [K].

With shadowy forests and with champains rich'd,
With plenteous rivers and wide-skirted meads,
We make thee lady. To thine and Albany's issue   65
Be this perpetual. — What says our second daughter,
Our dearest Regan, wife to Cornwall? Speak.

REG.   Sir, I am made of that self metal as my sister,
And prize me at her worth. In my true heart
I find she names my very deed of love;   70
Only she comes too short, that I profess
Myself an enemy to all other joys
Which the most precious square of sense possesses,
And find I am alone felicitate
In your dear Highness' love.

COR.   [*aside*] Then poor Cordelia!   75
And yet not so; since I am sure my love 's
More ponderous than my tongue.

LEAR.   To thee and thine hereditary ever
Remain this ample third of our fair kingdom,
No less in space, validity, and pleasure   80
Than that conferr'd on Goneril. — Now, our joy,
Although our last and least; to whose young love
The vines of France and milk of Burgundy
Strive to be interess'd; what can you say to draw
A third more opulent than your sisters? Speak.   85

COR.   Nothing, my lord.

LEAR.   Nothing?

COR.   Nothing.

63-4 *and . . . rivers* F¹; not in Q¹.   63 *champains* fertile plains.   *rich'd* enriched.
64 *wide-skirted* extensive.   68 *of that . . . sister* F¹; Q¹, K: "Of the selfe same
metall that my sister is."   *self* same.   69 *prize me* value myself.   70 *my very deed
of love* my love as it actually is in fact [K].   73 *Which . . . possesses* which the
most delicate test of one's sensibility can claim as joys [K].   *square* criterion (from
the carpenter's "square" used for exact measurements).   *possesses* Q¹; F¹: "professes."
74 *felicitate* made happy.   77 *ponderous* weighty. Her love is of heavier and
thus more precious metal than that of her sisters (F¹; Q¹, K: "richer").   80 *validity*
value.   82 *our last and least* youngest and smallest in stature (F¹; Q¹, K: "the last,
not least").   84 *interess'd* interested, closely connected (F¹, K: "interest," a variant
spelling).   89 *Nothing will* F¹; Q¹: "How, nothing can"; THEOBALD, K: "Nothing

LEAR.   Nothing will come of nothing. Speak again.

COR.   Unhappy that I am, I cannot heave   90
My heart into my mouth. I love your Majesty
According to my bond; no more nor less.

LEAR.   How, how, Cordelia? Mend your speech a little,
Lest it may mar your fortunes.

COR.   Good my lord,
You have begot me, bred me, lov'd me; I   95
Return those duties back as are right fit,
Obey you, love you, and most honour you.
Why have my sisters husbands, if they say
They love you all? Haply, when I shall wed,
That lord whose hand must take my plight shall carry   100
Half my love with him, half my care and duty.
Sure I shall never marry like my sisters,
To love my father all.

LEAR.   But goes thy heart with this?

COR.   Ay, good my lord.

LEAR.   So young, and so untender?   105

COR.   So young, my lord, and true.

LEAR.   Let it be so! thy truth then be thy dower!
For, by the sacred radiance of the sun,
The mysteries of Hecate and the night;
By all the operation of the orbs   110
From whom we do exist and cease to be;
Here I disclaim all my paternal care,

---

can."   92 *my bond* my bounden duty; as a daughter ought to love a father [K].
In larger terms it may be conceived of as the "bond of nature," that which links
child to father as it links mankind to God, all being part of a great and harmonious cosmic order.   96–7 *Return . . . honour you* in return I give you those
duties that are most fitting — obedience, love, and the highest honour. Thus Cordelia explains what she means by "my bond." "Duties" are "things that are due
to one, whether in act or feeling" [K].   100 *plight* pledge of faith in marriage.
103 *To love . . . all* Q¹; not in F¹.   109 *mysteries* secret rites (F²; F¹: "miseries";
Q¹: "mistresse"). *Hecate* goddess of the lower world, patroness of witches and magic.
110 *operation* astrological influence (upon man's character and fortunes). *orbs* stars.

Propinquity and property of blood,
And as a stranger to my heart and me
Hold thee from this for ever. The barbarous Scythian,   115
Or he that makes his generation messes
To gorge his appetite, shall to my bosom
Be as well neighbour'd, pitied, and reliev'd,
As thou my sometime daughter.

KENT.   Good my liege —

LEAR.   Peace, Kent!   120
Come not between the dragon and his wrath.
I lov'd her most, and thought to set my rest
On her kind nursery. — Hence and avoid my sight! —
So be my grave my peace as here I give
Her father's heart from her! Call France! Who stirs?   125
Call Burgundy! Cornwall and Albany,
With my two daughters' dowers digest this third;
Let pride, which she calls plainness, marry her.
I do invest you jointly in my power,
Preëminence, and all the large effects   130
That troop with majesty. Ourself, by monthly course,
With reservation of an hundred knights,
By you to be sustain'd, shall our abode
Make with you by due turns. Only we still retain
The name, and all th' additions to a king. The sway,   135
Revenue, execution of the rest,
Beloved sons, be yours; which to confirm,
This coronet part betwixt you.

---

113 *Propinquity* near relationship. *property* identity. Lear disclaims all kinship whatsoever [K].   115 *barbarous Scythian* By literary tradition from classical times the Scythians were regarded as the acme of all barbarians [K].   116 *makes . . . messes* eats his own children. *generation* children. *messes* portions of food. 117–18 *to my . . . neighbour'd* as closely hugged to my breast; so dearly loved [K].   119 *sometime* former.   121 *the dragon* A dragon was the traditional crest of the ancient British kings [K]. *wrath* object of anger.   122 *to set my rest* to rely with confidence and to the full. An idiom derived from the game of primero, meaning literally, to "make one's bet in reliance upon the cards in one's hand" [K].   123 *nursery* nursing, tender care [K]. *avoid* leave.   127 *digest* combine, incorporate. The word implies such perfect assimilation that no distinction shall hereafter be possible [K].   128 *Let pride . . . marry her* let her self-confidence be

KENT.   Royal Lear,
Whom I have ever honour'd as my king,
Lov'd as my father, as my master follow'd,   140
As my great patron thought on in my prayers —

LEAR.   The bow is bent and drawn; make from the shaft.

KENT.   Let it fall rather, though the fork invade
The region of my heart! Be Kent unmannerly
When Lear is mad. What wouldst thou do, old man?   145
Think'st thou that duty shall have dread to speak
When power to flattery bows? To plainness honour's
     bound
When majesty falls to folly. Reserve thy state;
And in thy best consideration check
This hideous rashness. Answer my life my judgment,   150
Thy youngest daughter does not love thee least,
Nor are those empty-hearted whose low sound
Reverbs no hollowness.

LEAR.   Kent, on thy life, no more!

KENT.   My life I never held but as a pawn
To wage against thine enemies; nor fear to lose it,   155
Thy safety being the motive.

LEAR.   Out of my sight!

KENT.   See better, Lear, and let me still remain
The true blank of thine eye.

LEAR.   Now by Apollo —

KENT.   Now by Apollo, King,

---

her dowry and (if it can) win a husband for her [K].   *plainness* frankness.   130
large effects splendid outward tokens [K].   135 *additions* titles and honours [K].
sway power of rule.   136 *the rest* everything else that pertains to royalty [K].
142 *make from* avoid.   143 *the fork* an arrowhead that, instead of a barb, has two
points like a pitchfork [K].   148 *Reserve thy state* retain thy kingly authority
(F¹; Q¹, K: "Reuerse thy doome").   150 *rashness* unthinking haste.   *Answer my
life* let my life be answerable for.   153 *Reverbs* reverberates. An old proverb says
that empty vessels have the loudest sounds.   154 *pawn* pledge (as the stake in a
wager).   155 *wage* wager, risk.   156 *motive* moving cause.   157 *still* always, forever.   158 *The true blank of thine eye* the mark at which thine eye directs itself
in accurate sight; the counsellor to whom thou dost look for sound advice.   The
"blank" is the white circle at the centre of the target [K].

Thou swear'st thy gods in vain.

LEAR.   O vassal! miscreant!   160

[*Lays his hand on his sword.*]

ALB., CORN. Dear sir, forbear!

KENT.   Do!
Kill thy physician, and the fee bestow
Upon the foul disease. Revoke thy gift,
Or, whilst I can vent clamour from my throat,   165
I'll tell thee thou dost evil.

LEAR.   Hear me, recreant!
On thine allegiance, hear me!
Since thou hast sought to make us break our vow —
Which we durst never yet — and with strain'd pride
To come between our sentence and our power, —   170
Which nor our nature nor our place can bear, —
Our potency made good, take thy reward.
Five days we do allot thee for provision
To shield thee from disasters of the world,
And on the sixth to turn thy hated back   175
Upon our kingdom. If, on the tenth day following,
Thy banish'd trunk be found in our dominions,
The moment is thy death. Away! By Jupiter,
This shall not be revok'd.

KENT.   Fare thee well, King. Since thus thou wilt appear,   180
Freedom lives hence, and banishment is here.
[*To* Cordelia] The gods to their dear shelter take thee,
    maid,
That justly think'st and hast most rightly said!

---

160 *vassal* A term of contempt. *miscreant* man without faith.   161 *Dear sir,*
forbear F¹; not in Q¹;   165 *vent clamour* utter outcries.   166 *recreant* traitor — one who proves false to his allegiance [K].   169 *strain'd* over-strained,
excessive, unnatural.   170 *to come . . . our power* to interfere with my power
to impose a sentence.   172 *Our potency made good* my royal power being in this
edict asserted and carried into effect [K].   173 *for provision* to enable thee to provide means [K].   174 *disasters* misfortunes (F¹; Q¹, K: "diseases").   180 *thus* as a
tyrant.   184 *approve* prove true, confirm.   185 *effects* deeds, consequences.   187
his old course as a faithful and plain-spoken subject [K].   188 *Here's* A singular
verb is common with two subjects, especially when the verb precedes [K].   192

[*To* Regan *and* Goneril] And your large speeches may
    your deeds approve,
That good effects may spring from words of love.   185
Thus Kent, O princes, bids you all adieu;
He'll shape his old course in a country new.   *Exit.*

                    Flourish. Enter Gloucester, *with*
              France *and* Burgundy; Attendants.

GLOU.   Here's France and Burgundy, my noble lord.

LEAR.   My Lord of Burgundy,
We first address toward you, who with this king   190
Hath rivall'd for our daughter. What in the least
Will you require in present dower with her,
Or cease your quest of love?

BUR.   Most royal Majesty,
I crave no more than hath your Highness offer'd,
Nor will you tender less.

LEAR.   Right noble Burgundy,   195
When she was dear to us, we did hold her so;
But now her price is fall'n. Sir, there she stands.
If aught within that little seeming substance,
Or all of it, with our displeasure piec'd,
And nothing more, may fitly like your Grace,   200
She's there, and she is yours.

BUR.   I know no answer.

LEAR.   Will you, with those infirmities she owes,
Unfriended, new adopted to our hate,
Dow'r'd with our curse, and stranger'd with our oath,

---

require ask. Not so imperative as in modern usage [K].   *present* immediate.   196
hold her so place such a value upon her.   198 *that little seeming substance* that
little creature, who seems to be something real, but is in fact a mere vain semblance of reality [K]. "Substance" is commonly used to indicate reality as opposed
to mere show or pretense. Lear is implying that since the love she had always
shown him was mere pretense, she is entirely a creature without substance.   199
piec'd attached, joined to it.   200 *fitly like* properly please.   202 *infirmities* defects of fortune, disabilities (not "physical weaknesses").   *owes* possesses.   204
Dow'r'd . . . oath with my curse as her sole dowry, and disowned by my oath of
rejection [K].

Take her, or leave her?

BUR.   Pardon me, royal sir.   205
Election makes not up on such conditions.

LEAR.   Then leave her, sir; for, by the pow'r that made me,
I tell you all her wealth. [*To* France] For you, great
        King,
I would not from your love make such a stray
To match you where I hate; therefore beseech you   210
T' avert your liking a more worthier way
Than on a wretch whom nature is asham'd
Almost t' acknowledge hers.

FRANCE.   This is most strange,
That she that even but now was your best object,
The argument of your praise, balm of your age,   ·   215
Most best, most dearest, should in this trice of time
Commit a thing so monstrous to dismantle
So many folds of favour. Sure her offence
Must be of such unnatural degree
That monsters it, or your fore-vouch'd affection   220
Fall'n into taint; which to believe of her
Must be a faith that reason without miracle
Should never plant in me.

COR.   I yet beseech your Majesty,
If for I want that glib and oily art
To speak and purpose not, since what I well intend,   225
I'll do't before I speak — that you make known
It is no vicious blot, murder, or foulness,
No unchaste action or dishonoured step,

---

206 *Election . . . conditions* to choose is impossible when the conditions of the
choice are so unfavourable.   208 *For* as for.   209 *make such a stray* stray so far
as.   211 *avert your liking* turn your preference.   214 *your best object* the main
object of your love and favour [K].   215 *argument* theme, constant subject.   216
trice moment.   217 *dismantle* strip off. "Favour" is conceived of in terms of clothing which had protected Cordelia but has now been stripped off.   220 *monsters it*
makes it a monster.   *fore-vouch'd* heretofore attested.   221 *Fall'n into taint*
suffered decay.   *her* emphatic. Of the two alternatives France chooses the second,
for the first is to him incredible [K].   225 *purpose not* have no intention of abiding
by what I have spoken.   227 *no vicious blot* no fault that leaves a stain on my

That hath depriv'd me of your grace and favour;
But even for want of that for which I am richer —   230
A still-soliciting eye, and such a tongue
As I am glad I have not, though not to have it
Hath lost me in your liking.

LEAR.   Better thou
Hadst not been born than not t' have pleas'd me better.

FRANCE. Is it but this — a tardiness in nature   235
Which often leaves the history unspoke
That it intends to do? My Lord of Burgundy,
What say you to the lady? Love 's not love
When it is mingled with regards that stands
Aloof from th' entire point. Will you have her?   240
She is herself a dowry.

BUR.   Royal Lear,
Give but that portion which yourself propos'd,
And here I take Cordelia by the hand,
Duchess of Burgundy.

LEAR.   Nothing! I have sworn; I am firm.   245

BUR.   I am sorry then you have so lost a father
That you must lose a husband.

COR.   Peace be with Burgundy!
Since that respect and fortunes are his love,
I shall not be his wife.

FRANCE. Fairest Cordelia, that art most rich, being poor;   250
Most choice, forsaken; and most lov'd, despis'd!
Thee and thy virtues here I seize upon.
Be it lawful I take up what's cast away.

---

moral character [K]. *murder, or foulness* Cordelia is thinking of such "offences" as
would be "unnatural" and "monstrous"; and, of these, murder and unchastity
("foulness") are the worst that she can imagine [K].   228 *dishonoured* dishonoura-
ble.   230 *for which* for want of which.   231 *still-soliciting* always begging favours
[K].   233 *lost me in your liking* ruined me in your regard [K].   235 *tardiness in
nature* natural reticence or slowness of speech [K].   239-40 *When it . . . entire
point* when it involves considerations that have nothing to do with the complete
and unqualified gist of the matter — i.e. with love that is purely and simply love
[K].   248 *respect and fortunes* considerations of social status and of money (F^1;
Q^1 K: "respects of fortune").

Gods, gods! 'tis strange that from their cold'st neglect
My love should kindle to inflam'd respect.   255
Thy dow'rless daughter, King, thrown to my chance,
Is queen of us, of ours, and our fair France.
Not all the dukes in wat'rish Burgundy
Can buy this unpriz'd precious maid of me.
Bid them farewell, Cordelia, though unkind.   260
Thou losest here, a better where to find.

LEAR.   Thou hast her, France; let her be thine; for we
Have no such daughter, nor shall ever see
That face of hers again. Therefore be gone
Without our grace, our love, our benison.   265
Come, noble Burgundy.

                Flourish. Exeunt Lear, Burgundy,
                [Cornwall, Albany, Gloucester, *and*
                Attendants].

FRANCE.   Bid farewell to your sisters.

COR.   The jewels of our father, with wash'd eyes
Cordelia leaves you. I know you what you are;
And, like a sister, am most loath to call   270
Your faults as they are nam'd. Love well our father.
To your professed bosoms I commit him;
But yet, alas, stood I within his grace,
I would prefer him to a better place!
So farewell to you both.   275

GON.   Prescribe not us our duties.

---

255 *inflam'd respect* passionate regard.　258 *wat'rish* (a) full of streams (b) diluted, weak.　259 *unpriz'd* unvalued by others.　260 *unkind* devoid of natural feeling.　261 *Thou losest . . . find* you lose this place in order to find a better place (France). "Here" and "where" are used as nouns.　265 *benison* blessing. 268 *jewels* objects held precious. *wash'd* by tears.　271 *as they are nam'd* by their right names. *Love* F[1]; Q[1], K: "Vse."　272 *professed* stored with mere professions of love [K].　274 *prefer* recommend.　276 *study* most zealous endeavour [K].　277 *content* please. Much stronger than in modern usage [K].　278 *At fortune's alms* when fortune was doling out petty charities, not bestowing bounteous awards [K].　279 *the want that you have wanted* the same lack of affection that you have shown. Your own lack of affection for your father deserves a similar lack of affection from your husband [K].　280 *plighted* enfolded. Their true feelings

REG.   Let your study
Be to content your lord who hath receiv'd you
At fortune's alms. You have obedience scanted,
And well are worth the want that you have wanted.

COR.   Time shall unfold what plighted cunning hides.   280
Who covers faults, at last shame them derides.
Well may you prosper!

FRANCE.   Come, my fair Cordelia.

                    Exeunt France *and* Cordelia.

GON.   Sister, it is not little I have to say of what most nearly
appertains to us both. I think our father will hence to-
night.   285

REG.   That's most certain, and with you; next month with us.

GON.   You see how full of changes his age is. The observation
we have made of it hath not been little. He always lov'd
our sister most, and with what poor judgment he hath
now cast her off appears too grossly.   290

REG.   'Tis the infirmity of his age; yet he hath ever but slen-
derly known himself.

GON.   The best and soundest of his time hath been but rash;
then must we look to receive from his age, not alone the
imperfections of long-ingraffed condition, but there-   295
withal the unruly waywardness that infirm and choleric
years bring with them.

REG.   Such unconstant starts are we like to have from him as
this of Kent's banishment.

---

are covered by many folds of cunning hypocrisy [K].   281 *Who covers . . . derides*
time, who at first conceals misdoings, at last exposes them to shame.   *covers* F¹;
JENNENS, K: "cover."   284 *will hence* will go hence. Such ellipsis of a verb of mo-
tion is very common [K].   288 *hath not* Q¹; F¹: "hath."   289-90 *with what poor
judgment . . . grossly* With cynical frankness Goneril admits that she and Regan
have spoken hypocritically and that Lear's love for Cordelia has been well deserved [K].   *grossly* crudely obvious.   293 *The best . . . but rash* even in the
prime of his life (time) he has been hasty (rash) in his actions.   295 *long-ingraffed
condition* a temperament that has been for a long time firmly imbedded in his
nature. "Graff" is an old form of "graft" [K].   *therewithal* therewith; together
with them.   296 *choleric* irritable.   298 *unconstant starts* sudden whims (a metaphor from horsemanship).   *like* likely.

GON.   There is further compliment of leave-taking between 300
        France and him. Pray you let's hit together. If our
        father carry authority with such disposition as he bears,
        this last surrender of his will but offend us.

REG.   We shall further think on't.

GON.   We must do something, and i' th' heat.   *Exeunt.* 305

◆◇◆◇◆◇◆◇◆◇◆◇◆◇◆◇

S C E N E I I . [*The* Earl of Gloucester's *Castle.*]

Enter [Edmund *the*] Bastard *solus,* [*with a letter*].

EDM.   Thou, Nature, art my goddess; to thy law
        My services are bound. Wherefore should I
        Stand in the plague of custom, and permit
        The curiosity of nations to deprive me,
        For that I am some twelve or fourteen moon-shines   5
        Lag of a brother? Why bastard? wherefore base?
        When my dimensions are as well compact,
        My mind as generous, and my shape as true,
        As honest madam's issue? Why brand they us
        With base? with baseness? bastardy? base, base?   10
        Who, in the lusty stealth of nature, take
        More composition and fierce quality
        Than doth, within a dull, stale, tired bed,

---

300 *compliment* ceremony, formality.   301 *hit together* agree in our conduct
toward him [K].   302 *carry authority . . . bears* shows such a mood in wielding his
power as he now manifests [K]. *disposition* F¹; Q¹, K: "dispositions."   303 *offend
us* cause us trouble.   305 *i' th' heat* while the iron is hot (an old proverb).
  I.II.   1 *Nature* The "Nature" which Edmund worships is conceived of as a force
independent of supernatural authority, governed only by its own mechanical laws.
These laws make no distinction between the legitimate child and the illegitimate,
and thus he feels that he need not respect the merely human law (custom) which
because of his bastardy would deprive him of rights to his father's estate.   3 *Stand
in . . . custom* occupy a position that exposes me to the grievous disabilities that
mere "custom" inflicts [K].   4 *curiosity of nations* nice distinctions which the
laws of nations make in defiance of nature and common sense [K]. *deprive me*
deprive me of the right to be my father's heir; disinherit me. Edmund is a

Go to th' creating a whole tribe of fops
Got 'tween asleep and wake? Well then,   15
Legitimate Edgar, I must have your land.
Our father's love is to the bastard Edmund
As to th' legitimate. Fine word — "legitimate"!
Well, my legitimate, if this letter speed,
And my invention thrive, Edmund the base   20
Shall top th' legitimate. I grow; I prosper.
Now, gods, stand up for bastards!

Enter Gloucester.

GLOU. Kent banish'd thus? and France in choler parted?
And the King gone to-night? prescrib'd his pow'r?
Confin'd to exhibition? All this done   25
Upon the gad? Edmund, how now? What news?

EDM.   So please your lordship, none.   [*Puts up the letter.*]

GLOU. Why so earnestly seek you to put up that letter?

EDM.   I know no news, my lord.

GLOU. What paper were you reading?   30

EDM.   Nothing, my lord.

GLOU. No? What needed then that terrible dispatch of it into
your pocket? The quality of nothing hath not such need
to hide itself. Let's see. Come, if it be nothing, I shall not
need spectacles.   35

EDM.   I beseech you, sir, pardon me. It is a letter from my

---

younger son, so that even if he were legitimate, he could not inherit his father's
lands [K]. 6 *Lag of* behind (in age). 7 *my dimensions . . . compact* my bodily
frame is as well constructed [K]. 8 *generous* befitting a nobleman. *true* sym-
metrical [K]. 9 *honest* chaste. *issue* child. 11 *lusty* vigorous. 12 *composition*
. . . *quality* strength of constitution and more energetic quality of body and mind
[K]. 14 *fops* fools, weaklings. 15 *Got* begotten, conceived. 19 *speed* prosper,
succeed in its purpose. 21 *top th'* CAPELL; F¹: "to' th' "; Q¹: "tooth." 23 *choler*
anger. *parted* departed. 24 *prescrib'd* limited, restricted (F¹; Q¹, K: "subscribed").
25 *exhibition* an allowance or pension (from his daughters). 26 *Upon the gad*
on the spur of the moment [K]. 28 *put up* pocket, conceal. 32 *terrible dispatch*
fearful haste in disposing. 33 *quality* nature. 36 *pardon me* excuse me (from
showing the letter).

brother that I have not all o'erread; and for so much as
I have perus'd, I find it not fit for your o'erlooking.

GLOU.   Give me the letter, sir.

EDM.   I shall offend, either to detain or give it. The contents,   40
as in part I understand them, are to blame.

GLOU.   Let's see, let's see!

EDM.   I hope, for my brother's justification, he wrote this but
as an essay or taste of my virtue.

GLOU.   (*reads*) "This policy and reverence of age makes the   45
world bitter to the best of our times; keeps our fortunes
from us till our oldness cannot relish them. I begin to
find an idle and fond bondage in the oppression of aged
tyranny, who sways, not as it hath power, but as it is
suffer'd. Come to me, that of this I may speak more. If   50
our father would sleep till I wak'd him, you should enjoy half his revenue for ever, and live the beloved of
your brother,

                                        "EDGAR."

Hum! Conspiracy? "Sleep till I wak'd him, you should
enjoy half his revenue." My son Edgar! Had he a hand   55
to write this? a heart and brain to breed it in? When
came this to you? Who brought it?

EDM.   It was not brought me, my lord: there's the cunning of
it. I found it thrown in at the casement of my closet.

GLOU.   You know the character to be your brother's?   60

EDM.   If the matter were good, my lord, I durst swear it were
his; but in respect of that, I would fain think it were
not.

---

38 *o'erlooking* inspection.   40 *to detain* by withholding.   41 *to blame* blameworthy, objectionable.   44 *essay* trial.   *taste* test.   45–6 *This policy . . . times*
the established order of society that forces the young to stand in awe of the aged
deprives us of the enjoyment of life when life is at its best. "Policy" (which often
means "cunning" or "strategic art") suggests that this order of society is a clever
trick on the part of the aged [K].   48 *an idle and fond bondage* a servitude to
which it is foolish to submit [K].   *idle* foolish.   *fond* foolish.   49–50 *not as it
. . . suffer'd* not by virtue of any power that it has but merely as the result of
our submission [K].   *suffer'd* submitted to.   52 *revenue* income.   54 *wak'd* Q¹;

GLOU.   It is his.

EDM.   It is his hand, my lord; but I hope his heart is not in the   65
          contents.

GLOU.   Hath he never before sounded you in this business?

EDM.   Never, my lord. But I have heard him oft maintain it to
          be fit that, sons at perfect age, and fathers declining, the
          father should be as ward to the son, and the son manage   70
          his revenue.

GLOU.   O villain, villain! His very opinion in the letter! Ab-
          horred villain! Unnatural, detested, brutish villain!
          worse than brutish! Go, sirrah, seek him. I'll apprehend
          him. Abominable villain! Where is he?   75

EDM.   I do not well know, my lord. If it shall please you to
          suspend your indignation against my brother till you
          can derive from him better testimony of his intent, you
          should run a certain course; where, if you violently pro-
          ceed against him, mistaking his purpose, it would make   80
          a great gap in your own honour and shake in pieces the
          heart of his obedience. I dare pawn down my life for
          him that he hath writ this to feel my affection to your
          honour, and to no other pretence of danger.

GLOU.   Think you so?   85

EDM.   If your honour judge it meet, I will place you where
          you shall hear us confer of this and by an auricular as-
          surance have your satisfaction, and that without any
          further delay than this very evening.

GLOU.   He cannot be such a monster.   90

F¹: "wake."   59 *casement* window opening on hinges.   *closet* private room.
60 *character* handwriting.   61 *matter* subject matter.   62 *in respect of that*
considering what that subject matter is. *fain* rather.   67 *sounded* probed
(a nautical metaphor).   69 *perfect age* prime of life.   75 *Abominable* unnatural, unfit for human society.   79 *run a certain course* be sure to proceed
without the risk of making a mistake [K]. *where* whereas.   81 *gap* breach.   83
feel my affection test my sentiments [K].   84 *pretence of danger* dangerous purpose.   86 *meet* fitting, proper.   87–8 *an auricular assurance* the evidence of actually hearing the facts.   88 *satisfaction* full information, confirmation.

EDM.   Nor is not, sure.

GLOU.   To his father, that so tenderly and entirely loves him.
         Heaven and earth! Edmund, seek him out; wind me into
         him, I pray you; frame the business after your own wis-
         dom. I would unstate myself to be in a due resolution.   95

EDM.   I will seek him, sir, presently; convey the business as I
         shall find means, and acquaint you withal.

GLOU.   These late eclipses in the sun and moon portend no
         good to us. Though the wisdom of nature can reason it
         thus and thus, yet nature finds itself scourg'd by the   100
         sequent effects. Love cools, friendship falls off, brothers
         divide. In cities, mutinies; in countries, discord; in pal-
         aces, treason; and the bond crack'd 'twixt son and
         father. This villain of mine comes under the prediction;
         there's son against father: the King falls from bias of   105
         nature; there's father against child. We have seen the
         best of our time. Machinations, hollowness, treachery,
         and all ruinous disorders follow us disquietly to our
         graves. Find out this villain, Edmund; it shall lose thee
         nothing; do it carefully. And the noble and true-hearted   110
         Kent banish'd! his offence, honesty! 'Tis strange.   *Exit.*

EDM.   This is the excellent foppery of the world, that, when
         we are sick in fortune, often the surfeit of our own be-

---

91–3 *Nor is . . . and earth* Q¹; not in F¹.   93–4 *wind me into him* worm your way
into his confidence for me [K].   95 *I would . . . resolution* I would abandon my
rank and fortune to have my doubts cleared up one way or the other [K].   96
presently at once.   *convey* manage.   97 *withal* with it; with the facts in the case
[K].   98 *late eclipses* Actual eclipses occurred in September and October of 1605,
a fact often used to date the play. Disturbances in physical nature in Shakespeare's plays often accompany or foreshadow disturbances in the state.   *late* recent.
99 *wisdom of nature* scientific reasoning, learning.   99–100 *reason it thus and thus*
explain it (the eclipses) in one way or another.   100 *nature* the natural world of
man.   *sequent effects* results which follow (the eclipses).   102 *mutinies* insurrec-
tions, riots.   103–4 *the bond . . . father* This should be compared to the "bond"
which Cordelia invokes at I.1.92.   104–9 *This villain . . . graves* F¹; not in Q¹.
105–6 *bias of nature* natural course or tendency. A figure from bowling. The "bias"
is the curve that the bowl makes in its course [K].   107 *Machinations* plottings.
hollowness insincerity.   109–10 *lose thee nothing* cause thee no loss. A back-
handed promise to reward his detective work [K].   112 *foppery* foolishness.
113–4 *surfeit . . . behaviour* the sickness being the result of the excesses of our

haviour, we make guilty of our disasters the sun, the
moon, and the stars; as if we were villains on necessity; 115
fools by heavenly compulsion; knaves, thieves, and treachers by spherical predominance; drunkards, liars, and
adulterers by an enforc'd obedience of planetary influence; and all that we are evil in, by a divine thrusting
on. An admirable evasion of whoremaster man, to lay 120
his goatish disposition to the charge of a star! My father
compounded with my mother under the Dragon's Tail,
and my nativity was under Ursa Major, so that it follows
I am rough and lecherous. Fut! I should have been that
I am, had the maidenliest star in the firmament twinkled 125
on my bastardizing. Edgar —

Enter Edgar.

and pat! he comes, like the catastrophe of the old com-
edy. My cue is villainous melancholy, with a sigh like
Tom o' Bedlam. O, these eclipses do portend these divisions! Fa, sol, la, mi.   130

EDG.   How now, brother Edmund? What serious contempla-
        tion are you in?

EDM.   I am thinking, brother, of a prediction I read this other
        day, what should follow these eclipses.

EDG.   Do you busy yourself with that?   135

own behaviour. "Surfeit" means "overeating"; fortune has had more of us than
she can stand and thus must grow sick.   115 *on* by.   116-17 *treachers* traitors.
117 *by spherical predominance* as the result of the predominance of some planet;
i.e. of its being the most powerful of all the planets at the moment of our birth
[K].   118-19 *influence* An astrological term for the effect of a planet on one's
nature and fortunes. It means literally "on-flowing," as if a mysterious force came
streaming down on us [K].   121 *goatish* lustful; the goat is a traditional symbol
for lechery.   122 *compounded* (a) created (b) came to agreement. *Dragon's
Tail* the constellation Draco, between Ursa Major (the Big Bear) and Cepheus.
123 *nativity* birth.   124 *Fut* Q¹; not in F¹.   126 *Edgar* Q¹; not in F¹.   127 *and pat*
and just exactly when he is needed (STEEVENS; F¹: "Pat"; Q¹: "and out") . *catastrophe* event which brings the plot to an end [K].   128 *villainous* miserable.
129 *Tom o' Bedlam* A common phrase for a vagabond maniac [K], or one who
pretended to be mad. "Bedlam" was Bethlehem Hospital, the London madhouse.
130 *Fa . . . mi* Edmund sings to himself in order to seem to be in a brown study
and unaware of his brother's approach [K] (F¹; not in Q¹).

EDM.   I promise you, the effects he writes of succeed unhappily:
       as of unnaturalness between the child and the parent;
       death, dearth, dissolutions of ancient amities; divisions
       in state, menaces and maledictions against king and no-
       bles; needless diffidences, banishment of friends, dissipa-   140
       tion of cohorts, nuptial breaches, and I know not what.

EDG.   How long have you been a sectary astronomical?

EDM.   Come, come! When saw you my father last?

EDG.   The night gone by.

EDM.   Spake you with him?   145

EDG.   Ay, two hours together.

EDM.   Parted you in good terms? Found you no displeasure in
       him by word or countenance?

EDG.   None at all.

EDM.   Bethink yourself wherein you may have offended him;   150
       and at my entreaty forbear his presence until some little
       time hath qualified the heat of his displeasure, which at
       this instant so rageth in him that with the mischief of
       your person it would scarcely allay.

EDG.   Some villain hath done me wrong.   155

EDM.   That's my fear. I pray you have a continent forbearance
       till the speed of his rage goes slower; and, as I say, retire
       with me to my lodging, from whence I will fitly bring
       you to hear my lord speak. Pray ye, go! There's my key.
       If you do stir abroad, go arm'd.   160

EDG.   Arm'd, brother?

---

136 *effects* several fulfillments of the prediction [K]. *succeed* follow   137-43
as of . . . come Q¹; not in F¹.   138 *dearth* famine.   140 *diffidences* cases of
mutual distrust [K].   140-1 *dissipation of cohorts* the breaking up of armed
troops [K].   142 *sectary astronomical* devotee of the astrological sect; a believer
in astrology. We may note that both Edmund and Edgar have no respect for
astrology [K].   143 *Come, come* A smiling protest against being regarded as "a sectary astronomical." Then Edmund becomes serious, as his question shows [K].
148 *countenance* behaviour, manner [K].   151 *forbear* avoid.   152 *qualified* modi-
fied, lessened.   153-4 *with the mischief . . . allay* his doing you bodily harm

EDM.   Brother, I advise you to the best. Go arm'd. I am no
        honest man if there be any good meaning toward you. I
        have told you what I have seen and heard; but faintly,
        nothing like the image and horror of it. Pray you, away! 165

EDG.   Shall I hear from you anon?

EDM.   I do serve you in this business.   *Exit* Edgar.
        A credulous father! and a brother noble,
        Whose nature is so far from doing harms
        That he suspects none; on whose foolish honesty   170
        My practices ride easy! I see the business.
        Let me, if not by birth, have lands by wit;
        All with me's meet that I can fashion fit.   *Exit.*

❖❖❖❖❖❖❖❖❖❖❖❖❖

        SCENE III. [*The* Duke of Albany's *Palace.*]

        Enter Goneril *and [her]* Steward [Oswald].

GON.   Did my father strike my gentleman for chiding of his
        fool?

OSW.   Ay, madam.

GON.   By day and night, he wrongs me! Every hour
        He flashes into one gross crime or other
        That sets us all at odds. I'll not endure it.   5
        His knights grow riotous, and himself upbraids us
        On every trifle. When he returns from hunting,
        I will not speak with him. Say I am sick.
        If you come slack of former services,

would not even be enough to satisfy his anger.   156–61 *I pray you . . . brother*
F¹; not in Q¹.   156 *have a continent forbearance* restrain yourself and keep out
of his presence [K].   158 *fitly* opportunely, at the proper time.   165 *the image
and horror* the horrible reality [K].   171 *practices* plots.   172 *wit* intelligence.
173 *All with . . . fit* everything, in my opinion, is proper for me that I can shape
to fit my designs [K].   *fashion fit* literally, make fitting by manipulation [K].
    I.III. 3 *By day and night* A mild oath.   4 *crime* offence. The word was less
specialized than in modern usage [K].   7 *On* for.

You shall do well; the fault of it I'll answer.   10

[Horns within.]

OSW.   He's coming, madam; I hear him.

GON.   Put on what weary negligence you please,
You and your fellows. I'd have it come to question.
If he distaste it, let him to our sister,
Whose mind and mine I know in that are one,   15
Not to be overrul'd. Idle old man,
That still would manage those authorities
That he hath given away! Now, by my life,
Old fools are babes again, and must be us'd
With checks as flatteries, when they are seen abus'd.   20
Remember what I have said.

OSW.   Very well, madam.

GON.   And let his knights have colder looks among you.
What grows of it, no matter. Advise your fellows so.
I would breed from hence occasions, and I shall,
That I may speak. I'll write straight to my sister   25
To hold my very course. Prepare for dinner.   *Exeunt.*

❖❖❖❖❖❖❖❖❖❖❖❖❖❖❖❖

SCENE IV. [*The* Duke of Albany's *Palace.*]

Enter Kent, [*disguised*].

KENT. If but as well I other accents borrow,
That can my speech defuse, my good intent

10 *answer* be answerable for.   13 *to question* to be discussed — an issue for
argument.   14 *distaste* dislike.   16–20 *Not to . . . abus'd* Q¹; not in F¹.   16 *Idle*
foolish.   19 *us'd* treated.   20 *With checks . . . abus'd* not merely with soothing
words, but, when they are seen to be deluded as to their position in life, with re-
bukes as well. Children are sometimes coaxed, sometimes scolded; the same treatment must be applied to childish old men [K].   *they* The antecedent is "old fools"
[K].   23 *Advise . . . so* give similar instructions to your fellow servants.   24–5 *I
would . . . speak* Q¹; not in F¹.   24 *breed . . . occasions* cause opportunities to
grow out of this; make an issue of it.   25 *straight* immediately.

May carry through itself to that full issue
For which I raz'd my likeness. Now, banish'd Kent,
If thou canst serve where thou dost stand condemn'd,   5
So may it come, thy master, whom thou lov'st,
Shall find thee full of labours.

Horns within. Enter Lear, [Knights,]
and Attendants.

LEAR. Let me not stay a jot for dinner; go get it ready. [*Exit
an* Attendant.] How now? What art thou?

KENT. A man, sir.   10

LEAR. What dost thou profess? What wouldst thou with us?

KENT. I do profess to be no less than I seem, to serve him truly
that will put me in trust, to love him that is honest, to
converse with him that is wise and says little, to fear
judgment, to fight when I cannot choose, and to eat no 15
fish.

LEAR. What art thou?

KENT. A very honest-hearted fellow, and as poor as the King.

LEAR. If thou be'st as poor for a subject as he's for a king, thou
art poor enough. What wouldst thou?   20

KENT. Service.

LEAR. Who wouldst thou serve?

KENT. You.

LEAR. Dost thou know me, fellow?

KENT. No, sir; but you have that in your countenance which 25
I would fain call master.

I.IV. 2 *defuse* disguise — literally, disorder [K].   3 *full issue* perfect result.   4
raz'd my likeness erased my true appearance (by assuming a disguise).   5 *canst
serve* canst manage to be engaged as a servant. Thus Kent explains why he has
"raz'd" his "likeness" [K].   8 *stay* wait.   11 *dost thou profess* is your profession
or calling.   12 *do profess* do claim.   13 *honest* honourable.   14 *converse* associate.   15 *judgment* God's judgment. *cannot choose* cannot help it.   15–16 *eat
no fish* i.e. be a good Protestant and thus a defender of the church and state in
Elizabethan times (an obvious anachronism).   25 *countenance* bearing — not
merely "face" [K].   26 *fain* be glad to.

LEAR.   What's that?

KENT.   Authority.

LEAR.   What services canst thou do?

KENT.   I can keep honest counsel, ride, run, mar a curious tale   30
         in telling it and deliver a plain message bluntly. That
         which ordinary men are fit for, I am qualified in, and
         the best of me is diligence.

LEAR.   How old art thou?

KENT.   Not so young, sir, to love a woman for singing, nor so   35
         old to dote on her for anything. I have years on my back
         forty-eight.

LEAR.   Follow me; thou shalt serve me. If I like thee no worse
         after dinner, I will not part from thee yet. Dinner, ho,
         dinner! Where's my knave? my fool? Go you and call my   40
         fool hither.   [*Exit an* Attendant.]

                  Enter [Oswald *the*] Steward.

         You, you, sirrah, where's my daughter?

OSW.   So please you —   *Exit.*

LEAR.   What says the fellow there? Call the clotpoll back. [*Exit*
         a Knight.] Where's my fool, ho? I think the world's   45
         asleep.

                        [*Enter* Knight.]

         How now? Where's that mongrel?

KNIGHT. He says, my lord, your daughter is not well.

LEAR.   Why came not the slave back to me when I call'd him?

KNIGHT. Sir, he answered me in the roundest manner, he would   50
         not.

---

30 *keep honest counsel* keep a secret when it is an honourable one [K]. *curi-*
ous elaborate, complicated. Kent implies that he is too outspoken to be a skillful
talker [K].   35 *to love* as to love.   40 *knave* boy. Often used as a term of famili-
arity — sometimes in affection, sometimes in contempt [K].   43 *So please you* if you
please — literally, may it be pleasing to you. Oswald obeys Goneril and "puts on
weary negligence" in his treatment of the King [K].   44 *clotpoll* stupid person —
literally, one who has a clod of earth for a head.   50 *roundest* plainest, most out-

LEAR.   He would not?

KNIGHT.   My lord, I know not what the matter is; but to my judgment your Highness is not entertain'd with that cere-
monious affection as you were wont. There's a great   55
abatement of kindness appears as well in the general
dependants as in the Duke himself also and your daughter.

LEAR.   Ha! say'st thou so?

KNIGHT.   I beseech you pardon me, my lord, if I be mistaken; for   60
my duty cannot be silent when I think your Highness
wrong'd.

LEAR.   Thou but rememb'rest me of mine own conception. I
have perceived a most faint neglect of late, which I have
rather blamed as mine own jealous curiosity than as a   65
very pretence and purpose of unkindness. I will look
further into't. But where's my fool? I have not seen him
this two days.

KNIGHT.   Since my young lady's going into France, sir, the fool
hath much pined away.   70

LEAR.   No more of that; I have noted it well. Go you and tell
my daughter I would speak with her. [*Exit* Knight.] Go
you, call hither my fool.   [*Exit an* Attendant.]

Enter [Oswald *the*] Steward.

O, you, sir, you! Come you hither, sir. Who am I, sir?

OSW.   My lady's father.   75

LEAR.   "My lady's father"? My lord's knave! You whoreson dog!
you slave! you cur!

OSW.   I am none of these, my lord; I beseech your pardon.

---

spoken.   54 *entertain'd* treated.   55 *wont* accustomed to be.   56 *appears* that
appears. The ellipsis of a relative pronoun in the nominative was formerly very
common and still occurs in colloquial speech [K].   63 *rememb'rest* remindest.
conception idea — that which has already occurred to me.   64 *a most faint neglect*
a very languid and neglectful manner [K].   65 *jealous curiosity* suspicious watch-
fulness about trifles [K].   66 *very pretense* true intention.

LEAR.   Do you bandy looks with me, you rascal?   [*Strikes him.*]

OSW.   I'll not be strucken, my lord.   80

KENT.   Nor tripp'd neither, you base football player?

                                         [*Trips up his heels.*]

LEAR.   I thank thee, fellow. Thou serv'st me, and I'll love thee.

KENT.   Come, sir, arise, away! I'll teach you differences. Away, away! If you will measure your lubber's length again, tarry; but away! Go to! Have you wisdom? So.   85

                                         [*Pushes him out.*]

LEAR.   Now, my friendly knave, I thank thee. There's earnest of thy service.   [*Gives money.*]

Enter Fool.

FOOL.   Let me hire him too. Here's my coxcomb.

                                    [*Offers* Kent *his cap.*]

LEAR.   How now, my pretty knave? How dost thou?

FOOL.   Sirrah, you were best take my coxcomb.   90

KENT.   Why, fool?

FOOL.   Why? For taking one's part that's out of favour. Nay, an thou canst not smile as the wind sits, thou'lt catch cold shortly. There, take my coxcomb! Why, this fellow hath banish'd two on's daughters, and did the third a blessing   95 against his will. If thou follow him, thou must needs

---

79 *bandy* literally, to "bat to and fro," as a ball in tennis [K].   80 *strucken* struck. 81 *football* an impromptu game, played both in the fields and the streets of towns, which was held in very low repute in Shakespeare's time.   83 *teach you differences* teach you to observe the proper distinctions of rank [K].   85 *wisdom* sanity. 86 *earnest* a small sum paid in advance to bind a bargain [K].   88 *coxcomb* The professional fool (the jester), whether in real life or on the stage, wore a hood or cap crested with a piece of red flannel, patterned after the comb of a cock [K]. 90 *were best* had better.   91 *fool* Q¹; F¹: "my boy," and gives the line to Lear. 93 *smile as the wind sits* take sides with the party that's in power [K].   95 *banish'd* By dividing his kingdom between Goneril and Regan Lear has made his daughters independent, and so he has lost them [K]. *on's* of his. *did the third a blessing* His banishment of Cordelia has made her Queen of France [K].   97

wear my coxcomb. — How now, nuncle? Would I had
two coxcombs and two daughters!

LEAR.   Why, my boy?

FOOL.   If I gave them all my living, I'ld keep my coxcombs   100
myself. There's mine! beg another of thy daughters.

LEAR.   Take heed, sirrah — the whip.

FOOL.   Truth's a dog must to kennel; he must be whipp'd out,
when the Lady Brach may stand by th' fire and stink.

LEAR.   A pestilent gall to me!   105

FOOL.   Sirrah, I'll teach thee a speech.

LEAR.   Do.

FOOL.   Mark it, nuncle.

> Have more than thou showest,
> Speak less than thou knowest,   110
> Lend less than thou owest,
> Ride more than thou goest,
> Learn more than thou trowest,
> Set less than thou throwest;
> Leave thy drink and thy whore,   115
> And keep in-a-door,
> And thou shalt have more
> Than two tens to a score.

KENT.   This is nothing, fool.

FOOL.   Then 'tis like the breath of an unfeed lawyer — you gave   120
me nothing for't. Can you make no use of nothing,
nuncle?

---

nuncle mine uncle.   100 *living* property.   102 *the whip* Whipping was the
punishment for fools who took too great liberties, as it was for naughty children
[K].   103-4 *Truth's a dog . . . and stink* Truth is whipped out of the hall; but
Flattery is allowed to keep a comfortable place by the fire, no matter how ill she
behaves [K].   104 *the Lady Brach* A contemptuous expression for a female dog,
like "Madam Bitch." Shakespeare often associates dogs with flattery (F¹; Q¹: "Ladie
oth'e brach"; STEEVENS, K: "Lady the Brach").   105 *pestilent gall* plaguy irritation.
111 *owest* ownest, dost possess.   112 *goest* walkest. An old proverb holds that he
is a fool who walks while his horse stands still.   113 *Learn . . . trowest* don't
believe everything you hear.   114 *Set . . . throwest* don't stake all your money
on a single throw of the dice.   116 *in-a-door* indoors.   120 *breath* speech.

LEAR.   Why, no, boy. Nothing can be made out of nothing.

FOOL.   [*to* Kent] Prithee tell him, so much the rent of his land
          comes to. He will not believe a fool.   125

LEAR.   A bitter fool!

FOOL.   Dost thou know the difference, my boy, between a bitter
          fool and a sweet fool?

LEAR.   No, lad; teach me.

FOOL.   That lord that counsell'd thee   130
                            To give away thy land,
                         Come place him here by me —
                            Do thou for him stand.
                         The sweet and bitter fool
                            Will presently appear;   135
                         The one in motley here,
                            The other found out there.

LEAR.   Dost thou call me fool, boy?

FOOL.   All thy other titles thou hast given away; that thou wast
          born with.   140

KENT.   This is not altogether fool, my lord.

FOOL.   No, faith; lords and great men will not let me. If I had
          a monopoly out, they would have part on't. And ladies
          too, they will not let me have all the fool to myself;
          they'll be snatching. Give me an egg, nuncle, and I'll
          give thee two crowns.

130–45 *That lord . . . snatching* Q¹; not in F¹. As he speaks these verses the Fool
places himself opposite Lear and at some little distance. He accompanies the
recitation with gestures [K].   130–1 *That lord . . . land* The fool implies that
nobody gave Lear such idiotic advice; Lear was his own foolish counsellor [K].
136 *The one* the sweet fool. He points at himself. "Motley" is the regular word for
the fool's ludicrously variegated costume [K].   137 *The other* yourself, "the bitter
fool." He points at Lear [K].   143 *monopoly* royal patent entitling me to be the
sole dealer in foolishness [K].   143–5 *they would have . . . snatching* the courtiers
who had helped me to secure the monopoly would insist on having their share —
and so would the court ladies. Monopolies, and the bribery or corrupt influence
by means of which they were often obtained, were constant subjects of satire in
Shakespeare's time [K].   147 *What two . . . be* The answer to the Fool's conundrum is obvious, since "crowns" was a common term for the two parts of the

LEAR.   What two crowns shall they be?

FOOL.   Why, after I have cut the egg i' th' middle and eat up the meat, the two crowns of the egg. When thou clovest thy crown i' th' middle and gav'st away both parts, thou 150 bor'st thine ass on thy back o'er the dirt. Thou hadst little wit in thy bald crown when thou gav'st thy golden one away. If I speak like myself in this, let him be whipp'd that first finds it so.

    [*Sings*] Fools had ne'er less grace in a year,   155
        For wise men are grown foppish;
      They know not how their wits to wear,
        Their manners are so apish.

LEAR.   When were you wont to be so full of songs, sirrah?

FOOL.   I have us'd it, nuncle, ever since thou mad'st thy daugh- 160 ters thy mothers; for when thou gav'st them the rod, and put'st down thine own breeches,

    [*Sings*] Then they for sudden joy did weep,
        And I for sorrow sung,
      That such a king should play bo-peep   165
        And go the fools among.

  Prithee, nuncle, keep a schoolmaster that can teach thy fool to lie. I would fain learn to lie.

LEAR.   An you lie, sirrah, we'll have you whipp'd.

FOOL.   I marvel what kin thou and thy daughters are. They'll 170 have me whipp'd for speaking true; thou'lt have me whipp'd for lying; and sometimes I am whipp'd for hold-

---

eggshell; but Lear wishes to let him make his joke. Conundrums are not meant to be guessed [K].   150–1 *thou bor'st . . . the dirt* you acted as foolishly as a man who carries his ass instead of letting it carry him. The Fool remembers a well-known fable [K].   153 *like myself* like a fool — if it is foolish for me to be so outspoken.   154 *that first finds it so* who first discovers that I have told you the truth. "So" is emphatic. The implication is that Lear has already made this discovery and that he, if anybody, should be whipped for folly [K].   155 *Fools . . . year* fools are now in less favour than at any other time.   156 *foppish* fool-ish — thus supplying the place of fools.   157 *their wits to wear* to use their in-telligence.   158 *apish* ridiculous, grotesque [K].   159 *wont* accustomed.   160 *us'd* practiced.   161 *mothers* F¹; Q¹, K: "mother."   165 *play bo-peep* be so childish as to hide himself — i.e. renounce his royalty [K].

ing my peace. I had rather be any kind o' thing than
a fool! And yet I would not be thee, nuncle. Thou hast
pared thy wit o' both sides and left nothing i' th' middle. 175
Here comes one o' the parings.

Enter Goneril.

LEAR.   How now, daughter? What makes that frontlet on? Methinks you are too much o' late i' th' frown.

FOOL.   Thou wast a pretty fellow when thou hadst no need to
care for her frowning. Now thou art an O without a 180
figure. I am better than thou art now: I am a fool, thou
art nothing. [*To* Goneril] Yes, forsooth, I will hold my
tongue. So your face bids me, though you say nothing.
Mum, mum!

> He that keeps nor crust nor crum,   185
> Weary of all, shall want some. —

[*Points at* Lear] That's a sheal'd peascod.

GON.   Not only, sir, this your all-licens'd fool,
But other of your insolent retinue
Do hourly carp and quarrel, breaking forth   190
In rank and not-to-be-endured riots. Sir,
I had thought, by making this well known unto you,
To have found a safe redress, but now grow fearful,
By what yourself, too, late have spoke and done,
That you protect this course, and put it on   195
By your allowance; which if you should, the fault
Would not scape censure, nor the redresses sleep,
Which, in the tender of a wholesome weal,
Might in their working do you that offence

---

176 *one o' the parings* Goneril, he argues, must have half of the King's wits, since
he parted with all his wits when he gave away his kingdom [K].   177 *frontlet* a
cloth worn across the forehead by ladies — hence, a frown.   180 *an O* a zero, without a digit to give it value.   185 *nor* Q¹; F¹: "not."   *crum* the soft part of the loaf
of bread   187 *sheal'd peascod* empty (shelled) peapod.   188 *all-licens'd* privileged
to say and do anything and everything [K].   190 *carp* complain, find fault.   191
rank excessive.   193 *safe* sure.   195 *put it on* encourage it.   196 *allowance* approval.   198–201 *Which . . . proceeding* and the acts of redress that we should find
necessary in our care for a sound condition of the state might, in their operation,
annoy you to an extent which, under other circumstances, would be shameful, but
which the necessities of the case would at this juncture force one to style discreet

| | Which else were shame, that then necessity | 200 |
| | Must call discreet proceeding. | |

FOOL.   For you know, nuncle,
             The hedge-sparrow fed the cuckoo so long
             That it had it head bit off by it young.
         So out went the candle, and we were left darkling.   205

LEAR.   Are you our daughter?

GON.   Come, sir,
         I would you would make use of your good wisdom
         Whereof I know you are fraught, and put away
         These dispositions which of late transport you   210
         From what you rightly are.

FOOL.   May not an ass know when the cart draws the horse?
         Whoop, Jug, I love thee!

LEAR.   Doth any here know me? This is not Lear.
         Doth Lear walk thus? speak thus? Where are his eyes?   215
         Either his notion weakens, his discernings
         Are lethargied — Ha! waking? 'Tis not so!
         Who is it that can tell me who I am?

FOOL.   Lear's shadow.

LEAR.   I would learn that; for, by the marks of sovereignty,   220
         Knowledge, and reason, I should be false persuaded
         I had daughters.

FOOL.   Which they will make an obedient father.

LEAR.   Your name, fair gentlewoman?

GON.   This admiration, sir, is much o' th' savour   225

procedure on our part [K].   203–4 *hedge-sparrow . . . young* The cuckoo lays its eggs in the nests of other birds.   205 *darkling* in the dark (like the dead hedge-sparrow; Lear is being destroyed by his daughters as the bird is destroyed by the cuckoo it has nourished).   208 *of your* F¹; Q¹, K: "of that."   209 *fraught* well furnished — literally, freighted [K].   210 *dispositions* states of mind; fits of capricious temper [K].   *which of late transport* F¹; Q¹, K: "that of late transforme."   213 *Jug* A nickname for "Joan" [K].   216 *notion* understanding. 220–3 *I would . . . father* Q¹; not in F¹.   220–2 *the marks . . . daughters* the outward signs of sovereignty, my knowledge, and my reason would all falsely convince me that I have daughters (which I see by your present action that I do not really have).   225 *admiration* pretending to wonder who you are [K].

Of other your new pranks. I do beseech you
To understand my purposes aright.
As you are old and reverend, should be wise.
Here do you keep a hundred knights and squires;
Men so disorder'd, so debosh'd, and bold   230
That this our court, infected with their manners,
Shows like a riotous inn. Epicurism and lust
Makes it more like a tavern or a brothel
Than a grac'd palace. The shame itself doth speak
For instant remedy. Be then desir'd   235
By her that else will take the thing she begs
A little to disquantity your train,
And the remainder that shall still depend
To be such men as may besort your age,
Which know themselves, and you.

LEAR.   Darkness and devils!   240
Saddle my horses! Call my train together!
Degenerate bastard, I'll not trouble thee;
Yet have I left a daughter.

GON.   You strike my people, and your disorder'd rabble
Make servants of their betters.   245

Enter Albany.

LEAR.   Woe that too late repents! — O, sir, are you come?
Is it your will? Speak, sir! — Prepare my horses.
Ingratitude, thou marble-hearted fiend,
More hideous when thou show'st thee in a child
Than the sea-monster!

---

228 *should* F¹, Q¹; Q², K: "you should." 229 *keep* support, maintain. 230 *disorder'd*
disorderly. *debosh'd* debauched. 231 *manners* conduct and character. 232 *Shows*
appears. *Epicurism* gluttony and riotous living. Shakespeare shows nothing in the
conduct of Lear's knights to warrant these accusations by Goneril. 233 *Makes* F¹;
ROWE, K: "Make." 234 *grac'd* honourable. *speak* call. 235 *desir'd* requested.
237 *disquantity* reduce in number. *train* retinue, followers. 238 *depend* attend
you as dependents; remain in your service [K]. 239 *besort* befit. 246 *that* to
him that. *O, sir . . . come* Q¹; not in F¹. 250 *Than the sea-monster* than any
monster of the deep [K]; he is not referring to any specific monster. 252 *parts*
qualities. Those critics who regard Goneril's complaints about the behaviour of
Lear's attendants as more or less justified fail to note the manifest purpose of
Lear's words here. That his Knights were well behaved is indicated also by the

ALB.   Pray, sir, be patient.   250

LEAR.   [*to* Goneril] Detested kite, thou liest!
         My train are men of choice and rarest parts,
         That all particulars of duty know
         And in the most exact regard support
         The worships of their name. — O most small fault,   255
         How ugly didst thou in Cordelia show!
         Which, like an engine, wrench'd my frame of nature
         From the fix'd place; drew from my heart all love
         And added to the gall. O Lear, Lear, Lear!
         Beat at this gate that let thy folly in   [*Strikes his head.*] 260
         And thy dear judgment out! Go, go, my people.

ALB.   My lord, I am guiltless, as I am ignorant
         Of what hath mov'd you.

LEAR.   It may be so, my lord.
         Hear, Nature, hear! dear goddess, hear!
         Suspend thy purpose, if thou didst intend   265
         To make this creature fruitful.
         Into her womb convey sterility;
         Dry up in her the organs of increase;
         And from her derogate body never spring
         A babe to honour her! If she must teem,   270
         Create her child of spleen, that it may live
         And be a thwart disnatur'd torment to her.
         Let it stamp wrinkles in her brow of youth,
         With cadent tears fret channels in her cheeks,
         Turn all her mother's pains and benefits   275

---

moderation of speech and manner shown by one of them in line 48*ff* [K].   255
worships honour. Abstract nouns are often pluralized when they refer to more
than one person [K].   256 *show* appear.   257 *frame of nature* the whole structure of my nature. The figure is that of a building that is thrown off its founda-
tion ("the fix'd place") by a powerful mechanical contrivance [K].   259 *gall* bit-
terness.   261 *dear* precious.   263 *Of . . . you* F¹; not in Q¹.   268 *increase* reproduction.   269 *derogate* blighted (by barrenness) — literally, deteriorated [K].   270
teem have offspring (a term usually applied to the reproduction of the lower
forms of life, such as insects and fish).   271 *spleen* malice and perversity. The
spleen was regarded as the source of these passions.   272 *thwart* perverse. *dis-
natur'd* unnatural.   274 *cadent* falling. *fret* wear.   275 *pains* care.

	To laughter and contempt, that she may feel	
	How sharper than a serpent's tooth it is	
	To have a thankless child! Away, away!	*Exit.*
ALB.	Now, gods that we adore, whereof comes this?	
GON.	Never afflict yourself to know more of it;	280
	But let his disposition have that scope	
	That dotage gives it.	

Enter Lear.

LEAR.	What, fifty of my followers at a clap?	
	Within a fortnight?	
ALB.	What's the matter, sir?	
LEAR.	I'll tell thee. [*To* Goneril] Life and death! I am asham'd	285
	That thou hast power to shake my manhood thus;	
	That these hot tears, which break from me perforce,	
	Should make thee worth them. Blasts and fogs upon thee!	
	Th' untented woundings of a father's curse	
	Pierce every sense about thee! — Old fond eyes,	290
	Beweep this cause again, I'll pluck ye out,	
	And cast you, with the waters that you lose,	
	To temper clay. Yea, is it come to this?	
	Ha! Let it be so. I have another daughter,	
	Who I am sure is kind and comfortable.	295
	When she shall hear this of thee, with her nails	
	She'll flay thy wolvish visage. Thou shalt find	
	That I'll resume the shape which thou dost think	
	I have cast off for ever; thou shalt, I warrant thee.	

Exeunt [Lear, Kent, *and* Attendants].

| GON. | Do you mark that, my lord? | 300 |

---

280 *more of it* F¹; Q¹, ᴋ: "the cause."   281 *disposition* mood.   287 *perforce* against my will.   288 *Blasts . . . thee* Fog and mist were thought to contain the seeds of pestilence [ᴋ]. *Blasts* lightning strokes of pestilence [ᴋ].   289 *untented* that are too deep to be probed; or, more exactly, to be searched with a "tent" — a slender roll of lint with which wounds are cleaned [ᴋ].   290 *fond* foolish.   292 *lose* waste — since these tears are of no avail [ᴋ].   293 *temper* moisten, soften. *Yea . . . this* Q¹, not in F¹.   294 *Ha* F¹; not in Q¹, ᴋ. *I have another* F¹; Q¹, ᴋ: "Yet haue I left a."   295 *comfortable* ready to comfort.   299

ALB.   I cannot be so partial, Goneril,
        To the great love I bear you —

GON.   Pray you, content. — What, Oswald, ho! [*To the* Fool]
        You, sir, more knave than fool, after your master!

FOOL.   Nuncle Lear, nuncle Lear, tarry! Take the fool with thee. 305
                A fox, when one has caught her,
                And such a daughter,
                Should sure to the slaughter,
                If my cap would buy a halter.
                So the fool follows after.   *Exit.* 310

GON.   This man hath had good counsel! A hundred knights?
        'Tis politic and safe to let him keep
        At point a hundred knights; yes, that on every dream,
        Each buzz, each fancy, each complaint, dislike,
        He may enguard his dotage with their pow'rs   315
        And hold our lives in mercy. — Oswald, I say!

ALB.   Well, you may fear too far.

GON.   Safer than trust too far.
        Let me still take away the harms I fear,
        Not fear still to be taken. I know his heart.
        What he hath utter'd I have writ my sister.   320
        If she sustain him and his hundred knights,
        When I have show'd th' unfitness —

                    Enter [Oswald *the*] Steward.

                            How now, Oswald?
        What, have you writ that letter to my sister?

OSW.   Yes, madam.

GON.   Take you some company, and away to horse!   325

---

thou shalt . . . thee Q¹; not in F¹.   305 *Take the fool with thee* An absolutely
perfect pun. The literal sense is obvious, but the phrase was a regular farewell
gibe: "Take the epithet 'fool' with you as you go!" [K].   308 *sure to* certainly
be sent to.   309 *halter* hangman's rope. Pronounced "hauter" to rhyme with
"after," pronounced "auter."   311–22 *This man . . . th' unfitness* F¹; not in Q¹.
313 *At point* fully armed.   314 *buzz* whisper, idle rumour.   315 *enguard* protect.   316 *in mercy* at his mercy.   318 *still* always.   319 *Not . . . taken* rather
than always live in fear to be attacked by some harm [K].   325 *company* escort.

Inform her full of my particular fear,
And thereto add such reasons of your own
As may compact it more. Get you gone,
And hasten your return. [*Exit* Oswald.] No, no, my lord!
This milky gentleness and course of yours,   330
Though I condemn not, yet, under pardon,
You are much more at task for want of wisdom
Than prais'd for harmful mildness.

ALB.   How far your eyes may pierce I cannot tell.
Striving to better, oft we mar what's well.   335

GON.   Nay then —

ALB.   Well, well; th' event.   *Exeunt.*

◇◇◇◇◇◇◇◇◇◇◇◇◇◇◇

S C E N E   V.
[*Court before the* Duke of Albany's *Palace.*]

Enter Lear, Kent, *and* Fool.

LEAR.   Go you before to Gloucester with these letters. Acquaint
my daughter no further with anything you know than
comes from her demand out of the letter. If your
diligence be not speedy, I shall be there afore you.

KENT.   I will not sleep, my lord, till I have delivered your   5
letter.   *Exit.*

---

326 *particular* own, personal.   328 *compact it more* make what I fear seem more
solid, more substantial [ĸ].   330 *milky . . . course* mild and gentle way that
you prefer.   331 *condemn not* f¹; ǫ¹: "dislike not"; POPE, ĸ: "condemn it not."
under pardon if you will pardon me for saying so [ĸ].   332 *at task* taken to
task, blameworthy [ĸ].   333 *harmful mildness* lenity that may prove injurious [ĸ].
335 *Striving . . . well* An old proverb, equivalent to "let well enough alone."
   I.v. 1 *these letters* this letter (from the Latin "litterae").   3 *demand . . .*
letter questioning as a result of her reading the letter.   8 *kibes* chilblains.   10
wit . . . slipshod intelligence will never have to wear slippers (because of the

FOOL. If a man's brains were in's heels, were't not in danger of
       kibes?

LEAR. Ay, boy.

FOOL. Then I prithee be merry. Thy wit shall ne'er go slipshod.   10

LEAR. Ha, ha, ha!

FOOL. Shalt see thy other daughter will use thee kindly; for
       though she's as like this as a crab 's like an apple, yet I
       can tell what I can tell.

LEAR. What canst tell, boy?   15

FOOL. She'll taste as like this as a crab does to a crab. Thou
       can'st tell why one's nose stands i' th' middle on's face?

LEAR. No.

FOOL. Why, to keep one's eyes of either side's nose, that what
       a man cannot smell out, 'a may spy into.   20

LEAR. I did her wrong.

FOOL. Canst tell how an oyster makes his shell?

LEAR. No.

FOOL. Nor I neither; but I can tell why a snail has a house.

LEAR. Why?   25

FOOL. Why, to put 's head in; not to give it away to his daugh-
       ters, and leave his horns without a case.

LEAR. I will forget my nature. So kind a father! — Be my horses
       ready?

FOOL. Thy asses are gone about 'em. The reason why the seven   30
       stars are no moe than seven is a pretty reason.

kibes) — because you have no intelligence.   12 *Shalt* thou shalt.   *kindly* The Fool
puns on "kindly" in the ordinary sense and in the sense of "according to her
nature" [K].   13 *a crab* a wild apple, very sour.   17 *on's* of his.   21 *her* Cordelia.   27 *horns* Shakespeare's audience were at liberty to recognize the ever-
lasting "horns" joke, for which they were on the alert. The Fool does not mean
to call Lear a cuckold; he simply accepts horns as the inevitable adornment of
married men [K].   *case* covering.   28 *forget my nature* cease to be a natural (kind
and loving) father.   30–1 *seven stars* the Pleiades.   31 *moe* more. Not a contrac-
tion of "more," but an independent formation from the same root [K].

LEAR.   Because they are not eight?

FOOL.   Yes indeed. Thou wouldst make a good fool.

LEAR.   To take't again perforce! Monster ingratitude!

FOOL.   If thou wert my fool, nuncle, I'ld have thee beaten for   35
          being old before thy time.

LEAR.   How's that?

FOOL.   Thou shouldst not have been old till thou hadst been
          wise.

LEAR.   O, let me not be mad, not mad, sweet heaven!   40
          Keep me in temper; I would not be mad!

                    [*Enter a* Gentleman.]

          How now? Are the horses ready?

GENT.   Ready, my lord.

LEAR.   Come, boy.

FOOL.   She that's a maid now, and laughs at my departure,   45
          Shall not be a maid long, unless things be cut shorter.

                                        Exeunt.

---

32 *not eight* The Fool has intentionally prepared a conundrum so obvious that the
answer is inevitable. Then he can make the point that he wishes: "Thou wouldst
make a good fool"; "You're good at this kind of foolery" [K].   34 *To tak't again*
to take back my royal powers. *perforce* by force.   41 *in temper* in a normal condition of mind [K].   45–6 *She that's . . . shorter* This bit of buffoonery is addressed to the audience. The Fool holds the stage for a moment before he follows
his master [K]. "Departure" and "shorter" would rhyme in Elizabethan pronuncia-
tion.

Act Two

❖◇

SCENE I.
[*A court within the Castle of the*
Earl of Gloucester.]

Enter [Edmund *the*] Bastard *and* Curan, *meeting.*

EDM.   Save thee, Curan.

CUR.   And you, sir. I have been with your father, and given
him notice that the Duke of Cornwall and Regan his
Duchess will be here with him this night.

EDM.   How comes that?   5

CUR.   Nay, I know not. You have heard of the news abroad —
I mean the whisper'd ones, for they are yet but ear-
kissing arguments?

EDM.   Not I. Pray you, what are they?

CUR.   Have you heard of no likely wars toward 'twixt the   10
Dukes of Cornwall and Albany?

EDM.   Not a word.

CUR.   You may do, then, in time. Fare you well, sir.   *Exit.*

EDM.   The Duke be here to-night? The better! best!
This weaves itself perforce into my business.   15
My father hath set guard to take my brother;

II.I. 1 *Save thee* God save thee.   7 *ones* "News" was originally a plural — "new
things" [K].   7–8 *ear-kissing* whispered.   8 *arguments* subjects of conversation.
10 *toward* impending.   10–11 *the Dukes* F¹; Q¹, K: "the two Dukes."   14 *The
better* so much the better.   15 *perforce* of its own accord.   16 *take* capture,
arrest.

And I have one thing, of a queasy question,
Which I must act. Briefness and fortune, work!
Brother, a word! Descend! Brother, I say!

Enter Edgar.

My father watches. O sir, fly this place!   20
Intelligence is given where you are hid.
You have now the good advantage of the night.
Have you not spoken 'gainst the Duke of Cornwall?
He's coming hither; now, i' th' night, i' th' haste,
And Regan with him. Have you nothing said   25
Upon his party 'gainst the Duke of Albany?
Advise yourself.

EDG.   I am sure on't, not a word.

EDM.   I hear my father coming. Pardon me!
In cunning I must draw my sword upon you.
Draw, seem to defend yourself; now quit you well. —   30
Yield! Come before my father. Light, ho, here! —
Fly, brother. — Torches, torches! — So farewell.

Exit Edgar.

Some blood drawn on me would beget opinion
Of my more fierce endeavour. [*Stabs his arm.*] I have seen
    drunkards
Do more than this in sport. — Father, father! —   35
Stop, stop! No help?

Enter Gloucester, *and* Servants *with
torches.*

GLOU.   Now, Edmund, where's the villain?

EDM.   Here stood he in the dark, his sharp sword out,

---

17 *of a queasy question* requiring delicate management [K].   18 *Briefness* decisive
speed, prompt action.   19 *Descend* Edgar is hiding in Edmund's chamber. See
I.II.158 [K].   23 *spoken 'gainst* committed yourself against the cause of (in the
quarrel between the two dukes).   26 *Upon his party* in support of his cause.   27
Advise bethink.   29 *In cunning* as a trick — in order that I may not seem to be
in collusion with you [K].   30 *quit you well* put up a vigorous defence [K].
34-5 *I have seen . . . sport* A wild gallant would sometimes stab his arm and
mix the blood with the wine when he drank his lady's health [K].   39 *Mumbling
of . . . the moon* Edmund adapts his story to his father's superstition [K].   40

             Mumbling of wicked charms, conjuring the moon
             To stand 's auspicious mistress.

GLOU.   But where is he?   40

EDM.   Look, sir, I bleed.

GLOU.   Where is the villain, Edmund?

EDM.   Fled this way, sir. When by no means he could —

GLOU.   Pursue him, ho! Go after. [*Exeunt some* Servants.] By
             no means what?

EDM.   Persuade me to the murder of your lordship;
             But that I told him the revenging gods   45
             'Gainst parricides did all the thunder bend;
             Spoke with how manifold and strong a bond
             The child was bound to th' father — sir, in fine,
             Seeing how loathly opposite I stood
             To his unnatural purpose, in fell motion   50
             With his prepared sword he charges home
             My unprovided body, lanch'd mine arm;
             But when he saw my best alarum'd spirits,
             Bold in the quarrel's right, rous'd to th' encounter,
             Or whether gasted by the noise I made,   55
             Full suddenly he fled.

GLOU.   Let him fly far.
             Not in this land shall he remain uncaught;
             And found — dispatch. The noble Duke my master,
             My worthy arch and patron, comes to-night.
             By his authority I will proclaim it,   60
             That he which finds him shall deserve our thanks,
             Bringing the murderous coward to the stake;
             He that conceals him, death.

---

stand's serve as his (Q¹; F¹: "stand").   46 *the thunder* F¹; Q¹, K: "their thunders." *bend* direct.   48 *in fine* finally.   49 *loathly opposite* bitterly opposed [K].   50 *fell* fierce. 51 *charges home* makes a home thrust at.   52 *unprovided* undefended. *lanch'd* pierced, wounded (Q¹; F¹: "latch'd").   53 *my best alarum'd spirits* all my best powers (energies) called to arms [K].   55 *gasted* struck aghast, panic-stricken. 58 *found — dispatch* when he is found let him be killed at once.   59 *worthy* honourable. *arch* patron, supporter.   62 *coward* F¹; Q¹, K: "caytife." *to the stake* to the place of execution; to his death. A figure derived from the stake to which one was fastened for execution by fire. Not to be taken literally [K].

EDM.   When I dissuaded him from his intent
        And found him pight to do it, with curst speech   65
        I threaten'd to discover him. He replied,
        "Thou unpossessing bastard, dost thou think,
        If I would stand against thee, would the reposal
        Of any trust, virtue, or worth in thee
        Make thy words faith'd? No. What I should deny   70
        (As this I would; ay, though thou didst produce
        My very character), I'ld turn it all
        To thy suggestion, plot, and damned practice;
        And thou must make a dullard of the world,
        If they not thought the profits of my death   75
        Were very pregnant and potential spurs
        To make thee seek it."

GLOU.   O strange and fast'ned villain!
        Would he deny his letter? I never got him.

                                        Tucket within.

        Hark, the Duke's trumpets! I know not why he comes.
        All ports I'll bar; the villain shall not scape;   80
        The Duke must grant me that. Besides, his picture
        I will send far and near, that all the kingdom
        May have due note of him, and of my land,
        Loyal and natural boy, I'll work the means
        To make thee capable.   85

                        Enter Cornwall, Regan, *and* Attend-
                        ants.

CORN.   How now, my noble friend? Since I came hither
        (Which I can call but now) I have heard strange news.

---

65 *pight* determined. *curst* angry.   66 *discover him* reveal his purpose.   67 *un-possessing* beggarly, incapable of holding title to property.   68 *reposal* placing.
70 *faith'd* believed.   72 *character* handwriting.   73 *suggestion* evil suggestion.
practice Synonymous with "plot."   74 *make . . . world* consider everyone to be
stupid.   76 *pregnant and potential* ready and powerful. *spurs* Q¹; F¹: "spirits."
77 *O strange* O unnatural (F¹; Q¹, K: "Strong"). *fast'ned* confirmed (in his villainy)
[K].   78 *got him* begot him (Q¹; F¹: "got him. Said he?").   79 *why* Q¹; F¹: "wher."
80 *ports* seaports.   84 *natural* Gloucester has both senses of the word in mind.

REG.	If it be true, all vengeance comes too short
	Which can pursue th' offender. How dost, my lord?
GLOU.	O madam, my old heart is crack'd, it's crack'd! 90
REG.	What, did my father's godson seek your life?
	He whom my father nam'd? your Edgar?
GLOU.	O lady, lady, shame would have it hid!
REG.	Was he not companion with the riotous knights
	That tended upon my father? 95
GLOU.	I know not, madam. 'Tis too bad, too bad!
EDM.	Yes, madam, he was of that consort.
REG.	No marvel then though he were ill affected.
	'Tis they have put him on the old man's death,
	To have th' expense and waste of his revenues. 100
	I have this present evening from my sister
	Been well inform'd of them, and with such cautions
	That, if they come to sojourn at my house,
	I'll not be there.
CORN.	Nor I, assure thee, Regan.
	Edmund, I hear that you have shown your father 105
	A childlike office.
EDM.	'Twas my duty, sir.
GLOU.	He did bewray his practice, and receiv'd
	This hurt you see, striving to apprehend him.
CORN.	Is he pursued?
GLOU.	Ay, my good lord.
CORN.	If he be taken, he shall never more 110

Edmund is his "natural son" and (he thinks) feels for him the "natural affection"
of a son for a father [K].   85 *capable* legally capable of inheriting. Gloucester
promises to legitimize the bastard by due process of law [K].   87 *strange news*
Q¹; F¹: "strangenesse."   95 *tended* attended (F¹; Q¹: "tends; THEOBALD, K: "tend").
97 *consort* company, gang (often used with contempt).   98 *though* if. *were ill
affected* had disloyal sentiments toward you [K].   99 *put him on* incited him to.
100 *expense* privilege of spending.   104 *assure thee* be assured.   106 *childlike
office* dutiful service befitting a son [K].   107 *bewray* reveal. *practice* plot.

Be fear'd of doing harm. Make your own purpose,
How in my strength you please. For you, Edmund,
Whose virtue and obedience doth this instant
So much commend itself, you shall be ours.
Natures of such deep trust we shall much need;   115
You we first seize on.

EDM.   I shall serve you, sir,
Truly, however else.

GLOU.   For him I thank your Grace.

CORN. You know not why we came to visit you —

REG. Thus out of season, threading dark-ey'd night.
Occasions, noble Gloucester, of some prize,   120
Wherein we must have use of your advice.
Our father he hath writ, so hath our sister,
Of differences, which I best thought it fit
To answer from our home. The several messengers
From hence attend dispatch. Our good old friend,   125
Lay comforts to your bosom, and bestow
Your needful counsel to our businesses,
Which craves the instant use.

GLOU.   I serve you, madam.
Your Graces are right welcome.   *Exeunt. Flourish.*

---

111 *of doing* lest he do.   111–12 *Make your . . . you please* form your own plan
for his capture and punishment, using my authority in any way that may seem
good to you [K].   114 *ours* in our service.   116 *seize on* take possession of (a
legal term).   119 *threading* making our way through [K].   120 *prize* importance
(F¹; Q¹, K: "poyse").   123 *differences* disputes.   *which* which letters.   124 *from*
when away from.   125 *attend dispatch* are waiting to be sent.   126 *Lay . . .
bosom* be comforted (in your own troubles).   127 *businesses* F¹; Q¹, K: "busines."
128 *craves . . . use* requires to be carried out without delay [K].
II.II. 1 *Art . . . house* are you a servant here?   8 *in Lipsbury Pinfold* between
my teeth. A "pinfold" is a pen for stray animals. There is no such town as "Lipsbury," which literally translated means "the region around the lips."   13–22 *A
knave . . . addition* Kent upbraids Oswald as a cowardly menial who parades as
a gentleman [K].   13 *broken meats* leftover table scraps.   14 *three-suited* This

◇◇◇◇◇◇◇◇◇◇◇◇◇◇◇◇

SCENE II. [*Before* Gloucester's *Castle.*]

Enter Kent *and* [Oswald *the*] Steward, *severally.*

OSW.   Good dawning to thee, friend. Art of this house?

KENT.   Ay.

OSW.   Where may we set our horses?

KENT.   I' th' mire.

OSW.   Prithee, if thou lov'st me, tell me.   5

KENT.   I love thee not.

OSW.   Why then, I care not for thee.

KENT.   If I had thee in Lipsbury Pinfold, I would make thee
        care for me.

OSW.   Why dost thou use me thus? I know thee not.   10

KENT.   Fellow, I know thee.

OSW.   What dost thou know me for?

KENT.   A knave; a rascal; an eater of broken meats; a base,
        proud, shallow, beggarly, three-suited, hundred-pound,
        filthy, worsted-stocking knave; a lily-liver'd, action-   15
        taking, whoreson, glass-gazing, superserviceable, finical
        rogue; one-trunk-inheriting slave; one that wouldst be a
        bawd in way of good service, and art nothing but the
        composition of a knave, beggar, coward, pander, and
        the son and heir of a mongrel bitch; one whom I will   20

---

seems to have been the regular allowance for a manservant [K].   *hundred-pound*
the minimum property qualification for one who aspired to be called a gentleman.
15 *worsted-stocking* Gentlemen wore silk stockings [K].   *lily-liver'd* white-livered;
i.e. having no blood in your liver, and therefore cowardly [K].   15–16 *action-*
taking going to law instead of meeting one's enemy in combat [K].   16 *glass-*
gazing always preening himself in a mirror [K].   *superserviceable* ready to
serve one's master in ways that are beyond the limits of honourable service
— even to the extent, Kent adds, of acting as a bawd [K].   *finical* fussy about
trifles [K].   17 *one-trunk-inheriting* all of whose possessions are contained in a
single box or trunk. To "inherit" means to "possess" [K].   18 *in way of good*
service if it comes in your day's work as a devoted servant [K].   19 *composition*
composite, compound,   20 *and heir* A fine touch! — not merely the "son," but
the "heir," inheriting all the mongrel's qualities [K].

beat into clamorous whining, if thou deny the least
syllable of thy addition.

OSW.   Why, what a monstrous fellow art thou, thus to rail on
one that's neither known of thee nor knows thee!

KENT.   What a brazen-fac'd varlet art thou, to deny thou know-   25
est me! Is it two days ago since I tripp'd up thy heels
and beat thee before the King? [*Draws his sword.*] Draw,
you rogue! for, though it be night, yet the moon shines.
I'll make a sop o' th' moonshine o' you. Draw, you
whoreson cullionly barbermonger! draw!   30

OSW.   Away! I have nothing to do with thee.

KENT.   Draw, you rascal! You come with letters against the
King, and take Vanity the puppet's part against the
royalty of her father. Draw, you rogue, or I'll so carbonado your shanks! Draw, you rascal! Come your ways!   35

OSW.   Help, ho! murder! help!

KENT.   Strike, you slave! Stand, rogue! Stand, you neat slave!
Strike!   [*Beats him.*]

OSW.   Help, ho! murder! murder!

Enter Edmund, *with his rapier drawn,*
Gloucester, Cornwall, Regan, Servants.

EDM.   How now? What's the matter? Part!   40

KENT.   With you, goodman boy, an you please! Come, I'll flesh
ye! Come on, young master!

GLOU.   Weapons? arms? What's the matter here?

CORN.   Keep peace, upon your lives!
He dies that strikes again. What is the matter?   45

---

22 *thy addition* the titles I have just given thee [K].   26–7 *tripp'd . . . beat thee*
F¹; Q¹, K: "beat thee, and tript up thy heeles."   29 *I'll make . . . o' you* I'll drill
you full of holes so that the moonlight can soak into you until you are a mere
sop — steeped in moonshine [K].   30 *cullionly barbermonger* vile fop, always dealing with barbers for the care of your hair and beard.   33 *Vanity the puppet*
Vanity was a stock figure in the older morality plays, and it survived in Elizabethan puppet shows. Kent equates the figure with Goneril.   34–5 *carbonado* slice
a piece of meat from.   37 *neat* foppish.   40 *Part* F¹; not in Q¹, K; K adds s.d:
"Parts them."   41 *goodman boy* A form of address to a presumptuous youngster
[K].   41–2 *flesh ye* give you your first taste of fighting.   47 *difference* dispute.
50 *disclaims in thee* renounces all claim to have produced thee [K].   54–5 *years o'*

REG.   The messengers from our sister and the King.

CORN.   What is your difference? Speak.

OSW.   I am scarce in breath, my lord.

KENT.   No marvel, you have so bestirr'd your valour. You
        cowardly rascal, nature disclaims in thee; a tailor made   50
        thee.

CORN.   Thou art a strange fellow. A tailor make a man?

KENT.   Ay, a tailor, sir. A stonecutter or a painter could not
        have made him so ill, though he had been but two years
        o' th' trade.   55

CORN.   Speak yet, how grew your quarrel?

OSW.   This ancient ruffian, sir, whose life I have spar'd
        At suit of his grey beard —

KENT.   Thou whoreson zed! thou unnecessary letter! My lord,
        if you'll give me leave, I will tread this unbolted villain   60
        into mortar and daub the walls of a jakes with him.
        "Spare my grey beard," you wagtail?

CORN.   Peace, sirrah!
        You beastly knave, know you no reverence?

KENT.   Yes, sir, but anger hath a privilege.   65

CORN.   Why art thou angry?

KENT.   That such a slave as this should wear a sword,
        Who wears no honesty. Such smiling rogues as these,
        Like rats, oft bite the holy cords atwain
        Which are too intrinse t' unloose; smooth every passion   70
        That in the natures of their lords rebel,
        Bring oil to fire, snow to their colder moods;
        Renege, affirm, and turn their halcyon beaks

---

th' F¹; Q¹, κ: "houres at the."   59 *zed . . . letter* The letter "z" is unnecessary because its sound is usually expressed by "s" [κ].   60 *unbolted villain* unsifted rascal; this fellow who is rascal through and through [κ].   61 *daub* plaster. *jakes*
privy.   62 *wagtail* a comically uneasy bird, so called from the spasmodic up-and-
down jerking of its tail. Oswald is too scared to stand still [κ].   68 *honesty* honourable character [κ].   69 *holy cords* sacred bonds of family affection [κ].   70
too intrinse tied in too close and intricate a knot (like the "Gordian knot") [κ].
smooth flatter.   72 *Bring* Q¹; F¹: "Being."   73 *Renege* deny. *halcyon beaks* It
was believed that the halcyon (kingfisher), if hung up, would serve as a weather-
vane, turning about so that its beak would always point in the direction from
which the wind comes [κ].

With every gale and vary of their masters,
Knowing naught (like dogs) but following.   75
A plague upon your epileptic visage!
Smile you my speeches, as I were a fool?
Goose, an I had you upon Sarum Plain,
I'ld drive ye cackling home to Camelot.

CORN.   What, art thou mad, old fellow?   80

GLOU.   How fell you out? Say that.

KENT.   No contraries hold more antipathy
Than I and such a knave.

CORN.   Why dost thou call him knave? What is his fault?

KENT.   His countenance likes me not.   85

CORN.   No more perchance does mine, or his, or hers.

KENT.   Sir, 'tis my occupation to be plain.
I have seen better faces in my time
Than stands on any shoulder that I see
Before me at this instant.

CORN.   This is some fellow   90
Who, having been prais'd for bluntness, doth affect
A saucy roughness, and constrains the garb
Quite from his nature. He cannot flatter, he!
An honest mind and plain — he must speak truth!
An they will take it, so; if not, he's plain.   95
These kind of knaves I know which in this plainness

---

74 *gale and vary* varying wind.   76 *epileptic* Oswald is trying to smile, but he is
so frightened that his face looks as if he were in a fit [K].   78 *Sarum* Salisbury.
79 *Camelot* the site of King Arthur's court. Tradition identified it with an
anciently fortified hill near Cadbury. In the moors in that vicinity there were
flocks of geese [K].   82 *antipathy* The phenomena which more recent science has
explained by the doctrine of "attraction and repulsion" were ascribed to "sym-
pathy and antipathy" in the nature of objects [K].   85 *likes* pleases.   92–3 *constrains the garb . . . nature* puts on by force the style of blunt sauciness in speech,
quite contrary to his real nature [K].   96 *plainness* outspoken manner of speech.
97 *ends* purposes.   98 *silly-ducking observants* obsequious parasites, who are
always making low bows after their ridiculous fashion [K].   99 *stretch . . .
nicely* exert themselves to be as precise and accurate as possible in performing
their duties [K].   *nicely* punctiliously.   100 *sincere verity* good faith (an
affected manner of speech).   101 *Under th' allowance* with the approval.   *aspect*

Harbour more craft and more corrupter ends
Than twenty silly-ducking observants
That stretch their duties nicely.

KENT.   Sir, in good faith, in sincere verity,   100
Under th' allowance of your great aspect,
Whose influence, like the wreath of radiant fire
On flickering Phoebus' front —

CORN.   What mean'st by this?

KENT.   To go out of my dialect, which you discommend so
much. I know, sir, I am no flatterer. He that beguil'd 105
you in a plain accent was a plain knave, which, for my
part, I will not be, though I should win your displeasure
to entreat me to't.

CORN.   What was th' offence you gave him?

OSW.   I never gave him any.   110
It pleas'd the King his master very late
To strike at me, upon his misconstruction;
When he, compact, and flattering his displeasure,
Tripp'd me behind; being down, insulted, rail'd
And put upon him such a deal of man   115
That worthied him, got praises of the King
For him attempting who was self-subdu'd;
And, in the fleshment of this dread exploit,
Drew on me here again.

KENT.   None of these rogues and cowards

(a) appearance (b) great power and authority. The "aspect" of a planet, in astrological terms, is its position in the heavens and the consequent influence, for good
or evil, which it exerts upon mankind.   102 *influence* force exerted by the planet
(another astrological term).   103 *Phœbus' front* the forehead of the sun. Kent in
this speech is parodying the style of a "silly-ducking observant."   105–8 *He that
beguil'd you . . . to't* I infer from what you have said that in the past some such
rascal as you describe has deceived you. If so, he was an out-and-out knave — and
that I will never be, even if I could induce you to lay aside your displeasure so
far as to beg me to be one [K].   111 *late* recently.   112 *misconstruction* mis-
understanding.   113 *compact* joined in a pact, in collusion (F¹; Q¹, K: "coniunct").
116 *That worthied him* as won honour for himself [K].   117 *For him . . . self-
subdu'd* for attacking one who submitted without a struggle [K].   118 *fleshment
of* bloodthirsty mood induced by.

But Ajax is their fool.

CORN.   Fetch forth the stocks!   120
You stubborn ancient knave, you reverent braggart,
We'll teach you —

KENT.   Sir, I am too old to learn.
Call not your stocks for me. I serve the King;
On whose employment I was sent to you.
You shall do small respect, show too bold malice   125
Against the grace and person of my master,
Stocking his messenger.

CORN.   Fetch forth the stocks! As I have life and honour,
There shall he sit till noon.

REG.   Till noon? Till night, my lord, and all night too!   130

KENT.   Why, madam, if I were your father's dog,
You should not use me so.

REG.   Sir, being his knave, I will.

CORN.   This is a fellow of the selfsame colour
Our sister speaks of. Come, bring away the stocks!

Stocks brought out.

GLOU.   Let me beseech your Grace not to do so.   135
His fault is much, and the good King his master
Will check him for't. Your purpos'd low correction
Is such as basest and contemn'dest wretches
For pilf'rings and most common trespasses
Are punish'd with. The King must take it ill   140
That he, so slightly valued in his messenger,
Should have him thus restrain'd.

---

120 *Ajax is their fool* the great hero Ajax is (by their own account) a fool in comparison with them — i.e. vastly their inferior [K].   121 *stubborn* fierce.   125 *malice* ill will. Not here used in the limited modern sense [K].   126 *grace and person.* As the King's messenger, Kent is to be treated with respect. Such a punishment would be not only an outrage on the King's "grace" (i.e. his royal honour) but a "personal" insult to him [K].   132 *should* would certainly.   134 *bring away* bring along; bring hither.   136–40 *His fault . . . with* Q¹; not in F¹.   137 *check* rebuke.   138 *contemn'dest* held in greatest contempt.   139 *pilf'rings* petty thefts.   140 *King must* Q¹; F¹: "King his Master needs must."   142 *answer* be answerable for.   145 *For . . . legs* Q¹; not in F¹.   149 *rubb'd* impeded, inter-

CORN.   I'll answer that.

REG.   My sister may receive it much more worse,
        To have her gentleman abus'd, assaulted,
        For following her affairs. Put in his legs. —   145

                    [Kent *is put in the stocks.*]

        Come, my good lord, away.

                    Exeunt [all but Gloucester *and* Kent].

GLOU.   I am sorry for thee, friend. 'Tis the Duke's pleasure,
        Whose disposition, all the world well knows,
        Will not be rubb'd nor stopp'd. I'll entreat for thee.

KENT.   Pray do not, sir. I have watch'd and travell'd hard.   150
        Some time I shall sleep out, the rest I'll whistle.
        A good man's fortune may grow out at heels.
        Give you good morrow!

GLOU.   The Duke's to blame in this; 'twill be ill taken.   *Exit.*

KENT.   Good King, that must approve the common saw,   155
        Thou out of heaven's benediction com'st
        To the warm sun!
        Approach, thou beacon to this under globe,
        That by thy comfortable beams I may
        Peruse this letter. Nothing almost sees miracles   160
        But misery. I know 'tis from Cordelia,
        Who hath most fortunately been inform'd
        Of my obscured course — and [*reads*] "shall find time
        From this enormous state, seeking to give

---

fered with. This sense comes from bowling. A "rub" is anything that hinders or
deflects the course of the bowl [K]   150 *watch'd* gone without sleep.   152 *A good
. . . heels* A proverb meaning that it is no disgrace to decline in fortune.   154
to blame blameworthy.   155 *must approve . . . saw* art fated, it seems to ex-
emplify the familiar saying [K].   156–7 *Thou out . . . sun* The proverb describes
bad judgment by the figure of one who, on a hot day, leaves a comfortable seat
in the shade for a place in the sun [K].   159 *comfortable* comforting, helpful.
160–1 *Nothing . . . misery* for, when we are in despair, any relief seems miracu-
lous [K].   163 *obscured course* course of action in this disguise [K].   164 *this
enormous state* the present anomalous condition of the realm [K].

Losses their remedies" — All weary and o'erwatch'd,   165
Take vantage, heavy eyes, not to behold
This shameful lodging.
Fortune, good night; smile once more, turn thy wheel.

Sleeps.

❖❖❖❖❖❖❖❖❖❖❖❖❖❖❖

[SCENE III. *The open country.*]

Enter Edgar.

EDG.   I heard myself proclaim'd,
And by the happy hollow of a tree
Escap'd the hunt. No port is free, no place
That guard and most unusual vigilance
Does not attend my taking. Whiles I may scape,   5
I will preserve myself; and am bethought
To take the basest and most poorest shape
That ever penury, in contempt of man,
Brought near to beast. My face I'll grime with filth,
Blanket my loins, elf all my hairs in knots,   10
And with presented nakedness outface
The winds and persecutions of the sky.
The country gives me proof and precedent
Of Bedlam beggars, who, with roaring voices,
Strike in their numb'd and mortified bare arms   15
Pins, wooden pricks, nails, sprigs of rosemary;

165 *o'erwatch'd* worn out by lack of sleep.   166 *vantage* advantage.   *heavy* drowsy.   167 *lodging* sleeping quarters for the night. He will take advantage of sleep so as to avoid seeing the stocks.   168 *wheel* the proverbial wheel of fortune.
     II.III. 2 *happy* fortunate (as a hiding place).   5 *attend my taking* wait to capture me.   6 *am bethought* have thought of the idea.   8 *in contempt of man* as if to show how contemptible a creature a man may be [K].   10 *elf . . . in knots* Matted and tangled locks of hair — due to neglect and filthy habits — were ascribed to the action of mischievous elves and hence called "elflocks" [K].   *hairs* F[1]; Q[1], K: "hair."   11 *presented* fully exposed.   *outface* defy.   13 *proof* example.   15 *mortified* deadened by hardship and exposure [K].   17 *object* spectacle.   *low* lowly, humble.   18 *pelting* paltry, insignificant.   *sheepcotes, and mills* both of

And with this horrible object, from low farms,
Poor pelting villages, sheepcotes, and mills,
Sometime with lunatic bans, sometime with prayers,
Enforce their charity. "Poor Turlygod! poor Tom!"   20
That's something yet! Edgar I nothing am.   *Exit.*

◇◇◇◇◇◇◇◇◇◇◇◇◇◇◇

[SCENE IV.
Before Gloucester's *Castle;* Kent *in the stocks.*]

Enter Lear, Fool, *and* Gentleman.

LEAR.   'Tis strange that they should so depart from home,
And not send back my messenger.

GENT.   As I learn'd,
The night before there was no purpose in them
Of this remove.

KENT.   Hail to thee, noble master!

LEAR.   Ha!   5
Mak'st thou this shame thy pastime?

KENT.   No, my lord.

FOOL.   Ha, ha! look! he wears cruel garters. Horses are tied by
the heads, dogs and bears by th' neck, monkeys by th'
loins, and men by th' legs. When a man's over-lusty at
legs, then he wears wooden nether-stocks.   10

---

which were often distant from any village [K].   19 *bans* curses.   20 *Poor . . .
Tom* Edgar practises the Bedlam beggar's whine. "Turlygod" seems to have been
a name by which such a beggar sometimes called himself, but it occurs nowhere
else [K].   21 *That's something . . . nothing am* as Poor Tom there is, after all,
some hope for me. In my real character as Edgar, I am as good as dead — i.e. I
have no chance of preserving my life [K].

II.IV. 4 *remove* change of residence.   7 *cruel* with a pun on "crewel," a kind
of worsted yarn used for garters.   8 *heads* F¹; Q¹: "heeles"; K: "head."   9-10 *over-
lusty at legs* too vigorous in using his legs; too much of a vagabond [K].   10
nether-stocks stockings. Overstocks (upper stocks) were breeches [K].

LEAR.   What's he that hath so much thy place mistook
         To set thee here?

KENT.   It is both he and she —
         Your son and daughter.

LEAR.   No.

KENT.   Yes.   15

LEAR.   No, I say.

KENT.   I say yea.

LEAR.   No, no, they would not!

KENT.   Yes, they have.

LEAR.   By Jupiter, I swear no!   20

KENT.   By Juno, I swear ay!

LEAR.   They durst not do't;
         They would not, could not do't. 'Tis worse than murder
         To do upon respect such violent outrage.
         Resolve me with all modest haste which way
         Thou mightst deserve or they impose this usage,   25
         Coming from us.

KENT.   My lord, when at their home
         I did commend your Highness' letters to them,
         Ere I was risen from the place that show'd
         My duty kneeling, came there a reeking post,
         Stew'd in his haste, half breathless, panting forth   30
         From Goneril his mistress salutations;
         Deliver'd letters, spite of intermission,
         Which presently they read; on whose contents,
         They summon'd up their meiny, straight took horse,
         Commanded me to follow and attend   35

---

11 *place* position (as the King's messenger).   18–19 *No, no . . . have* Q¹; not in F¹.
21 *By . . . ay* F¹; not in Q¹.   23 *upon respect* against the respect due to the King [K].
24 *Resolve me* explain to me.   *modest* moderate.   26 *from us* from me, the King.
27 *commend* deliver.   30 *Stew'd* steaming.   *panting* Q¹; F¹: "painting."   32 *spite
of intermission* in spite of the fact that it interrupted the audience they had
granted me [K].   34 *meiny* household servants.   *straight* immediately.   40 *Display'd so saucily* made such an impudent exhibition of himself [K].   41 *more
man than wit* more courage than common sense [K].   *drew* my sword.   45–53
Winter's . . . a year F¹; not in Q¹.   42 *rais'd* aroused.   48 *bags* moneybags.

The leisure of their answer, gave me cold looks,
And meeting here the other messenger,
Whose welcome I perceiv'd had poison'd mine —
Being the very fellow which of late
Display'd so saucily against your Highness —   40
Having more man than wit about me, drew.
He rais'd the house with loud and coward cries.
Your son and daughter found this trespass worth
The shame which here it suffers.

FOOL.   Winter's not gone yet, if the wild geese fly that way.   45
                Fathers that wear rags
                    Do make their children blind;
                But fathers that bear bags
                    Shall see their children kind.
                Fortune, that arrant whore,   50
                    Ne'er turns the key to th' poor.
          But for all this, thou shalt have as many dolours for thy
          daughters as thou canst tell in a year.

LEAR.   O, how this mother swells up toward my heart!
          Hysterica passio! Down, thou climbing sorrow!   55
          Thy element's below! Where is this daughter?

KENT.   With the Earl, sir, here within.

LEAR.   Follow me not;
          Stay here.   *Exit.*

GENT.   Made you no more offence but what you speak of?

KENT.   None.   60
          How chance the King comes with so small a number?

FOOL.   An thou hadst been set i' th' stocks for that question,
          thou'dst well deserv'd it.

---

50 *Fortune . . . whore* Fortune is often called a harlot because she shows favour
to every man and is constant to none [K].   51 *turns the key* opens the door.
52 *dolours* sorrows (with a pun on "dollars").   53 *tell* (a) recount (b) count up.
54 *this mother* The "mother" was the popular name for "hysterica passio" —
"hysterical suffering," hysteria. Lear describes the symptoms — a feeling of distress
rising from below toward the heart. Thence it often ascends into the throat with
the sensation of choking — called "the hysteric ball" [K].   56 *element* proper
place.   63 *thou'dst well deserv'd it* because it's a foolish question, since the
answer is so obvious [K].

KENT.   Why, fool?

FOOL.   We'll set thee to school to an ant, to teach thee there's   65
          no labouring i' th' winter. All that follow their noses are
          led by their eyes but blind men, and there's not a nose
          among twenty but can smell him that's stinking. Let go
          thy hold when a great wheel runs down a hill, lest it
          break thy neck with following it; but the great one that   70
          goes upward, let him draw thee after. When a wise man
          gives thee better counsel, give me mine again. I would
          have none but knaves follow it, since a fool gives it.

               That sir which serves and seeks for gain,
                    And follows but for form,   75
               Will pack when it begins to rain
                    And leave thee in the storm.
               But I will tarry; the fool will stay,
                    And let the wise man fly.
               The knave turns fool that runs away;   80
                    The fool no knave, perdy.

KENT.   Where learn'd you this, fool?

FOOL.   Not i' th' stocks, fool.

                    Enter Lear *and* Gloucester.

LEAR.   Deny to speak with me? They are sick? they are weary?
          They have travell'd all the night? Mere fetches —   85
          The images of revolt and flying off!
          Fetch me a better answer.

65–73 *We'll set . . . gives it* In a series of brief parables the Fool explains that
Lear's fortunes are in a bad way, and that it is therefore not strange that he
comes with so small a retinue [K].   66 *All that follow their noses* To "follow
one's nose" is an old jocose idiom (still in use) for "to go straight ahead in the
direction in which one's nose points." "All persons who follow a straight course
of judgment accept the evidence of their eyes, if they have any eyes. And even
the blind can follow their noses — can use the sense of smell as a guide. In the
present instance, then, even a blind man can discover the facts of the case (the
desperate condition of the King's fortunes), for among a score of noses there's
surely not one that is "not good enough to recognize a stench" [K].   75 *form*
show.   76 *pack* run away.   80–1 *The knave . . . no knave* the fellow that for-
sakes his master is (from the point of view of the higher wisdom) a fool, since

GLOU.   My dear lord,
         You know the fiery quality of the Duke,
         How unremovable and fix'd he is
         In his own course.   90

LEAR.   Vengeance! plague! death! confusion!
         Fiery? What quality? Why, Gloucester, Gloucester,
         I'ld speak with the Duke of Cornwall and his wife.

GLOU.   Well, my good lord, I have inform'd them so.

LEAR.   Inform'd them? Dost thou understand me, man?   95

GLOU.   Ay, my good lord.

LEAR.   The King would speak with Cornwall; the dear father
         Would with his daughter speak, commands her service.
         Are they inform'd of this? My breath and blood!
         Fiery? the fiery Duke? Tell the hot Duke that —   100
         No, but not yet! May be he is not well.
         Infirmity doth still neglect all office
         Whereto our health is bound. We are not ourselves
         When nature, being oppress'd, commands the mind
         To suffer with the body. I'll forbear;   105
         And am fallen out with my more headier will,
         To take the indispos'd and sickly fit
         For the sound man. — Death on my state! Wherefore
         Should he sit here? This act persuades me
         That this remotion of the Duke and her   110
         Is practice only. Give me my servant forth.
         Go tell the Duke and 's wife I'ld speak with them —
         Now, presently. Bid them come forth and hear me,

---

true wisdom implies fidelity; and the fool who, like me, remains faithful is, at all
events, no knave [K].   81 *perdy* assuredly.   84 *Deny* refuse.   85 *fetches* pretexts,
excuses.   86 *images* plainest possible signs [K].   *revolt and flying off* To explain
or emphasize a word by adding a synonym is one of the commonest of rhetorical
devices [K].   88 *quality* nature, character.   95-5 *Well . . . man* F¹; not in Q¹.
98 *commands her service* Q¹; F¹: "commands, tends, seruice."   99 *My breath and
blood* Another oath, used merely as a passionate exclamation [K]   (F¹; not in Q¹).
102 *neglect* omit, leave undone.   *office* service, duty.   106 *fallen out* angry.   *more
headier* too impulsive.   *will* impulse.   108 *state* royal power.   109 *he* Kent.
110 *remotion* keeping away from me; avoidance of an interview [K].   111 *practice*
trickery.   *forth* release (from the stocks).   113 *presently* at once.

	Or at their chamber door I'll beat the drum	
	Till it cry sleep to death.	115
GLOU.	I would have all well betwixt you. *Exit.*	
LEAR.	O me, my heart, my rising heart! But down!	
FOOL.	Cry to it, nuncle, as the cockney did to the eels when she	
	put 'em i' th' paste alive. She knapp'd 'em o' th' cox-	
	combs with a stick and cried "Down, wantons, down!"	120
	'Twas her brother that, in pure kindness to his horse,	
	buttered his hay.	

Enter Cornwall, Regan, Gloucester,
Servants.

LEAR.	Good morrow to you both.	
CORN.	Hail to your Grace!	
	Kent *here set at liberty.*	
REG.	I am glad to see your Highness.	
LEAR.	Regan, I think you are; I know what reason	125
	I have to think so. If thou shouldst not be glad,	
	I would divorce me from thy mother's tomb,	
	Sepulchring an adultress. [*To* Kent] O, are you free?	
	Some other time for that. — Beloved Regan,	
	Thy sister's naught. O Regan, she hath tied	130
	Sharp-tooth'd unkindness, like a vulture, here!	

[*Lays his hand on his heart.*]

	I can scarce speak to thee. Thou'lt not believe
	With how deprav'd a quality — O Regan!
REG.	I pray you, sir, take patience. I have hope

---

115 *cry sleep to death* make sleep impossible by its din [ᴋ].   118 *Cockney* city-dweller (unfamiliar with the preparation of eels). The word also may mean "spoiled child," "pampered darling," "cook," or "Londoner."   119 *paste* pastry, pie shell.   *knapp'd* beat (F¹; Q¹: "rapt").   119–20 *coxcombs* heads.   120 *wantons* naughty, frisky things.   121 *brother* a member of the same family of fools; another fool of the same breed [ᴋ].   128 *Sepulchring* as being the tomb of.   130 *naught* wicked.   131 *like a vulture* Such allusions to the torment of Prometheus are common [ᴋ].   133 *quality* character, disposition.   135–6 *You less . . . duty* she does not come short in doing her duty to you. The trouble is, that you can-

     You less know how to value her desert   135
     Than she to scant her duty.

LEAR.   Say, how is that?

REG.   I cannot think my sister in the least
     Would fail her obligation. If, sir, perchance
     She have restrain'd the riots of your followers,
     'Tis on such ground, and to such wholesome end,   140
     As clears her from all blame.

LEAR.   My curses on her!

REG.   O, sir, you are old!
     Nature in you stands on the very verge
     Of her confine. You should be rul'd, and led
     By some discretion that discerns your state   145
     Better than you yourself. Therefore I pray you
     That to our sister you do make return;
     Say you have wrong'd her, sir.

LEAR.   Ask her forgiveness?
     Do you but mark how this becomes the house:
     "Dear daughter, I confess that I am old.   [*Kneels.*] 150
     Age is unnecessary. On my knees I beg
     That you'll vouchsafe me raiment, bed, and food."

REG.   Good sir, no more! These are unsightly tricks.
     Return you to my sister.

LEAR.   [*rises*]   Never, Regan!
     She hath abated me of half my train;   155
     Look'd black upon me; struck me with her tongue,
     Most serpent-like, upon the very heart.
     All the stor'd vengeances of heaven fall

---

not appreciate her merits [K].   136 *scant* This repeats the negative idea, but the double negative does not make an affirmative. In modern English we should say "to do her duty" [K].   136–41 *Say . . . all blame* F[1]; not in Q[1].   143–4 *Nature . . . her confine* your life is at the very end of its assigned period; you are old and ready for death.   145 *some discretion . . . state* some understanding person who understands your condition of mind.   147 *make return* go back again.   149 *becomes the house* befits family relations. Spoken with bitter irony; fathers would not kneel to their children in any normal family [K].   151 *Age is unnecessary* old folk are of no use in the world [K].   155 *abated* deprived, curtailed.

On her ingrateful top! Strike her young bones,
You taking airs, with lameness!

CORN.   Fie, sir, fie!   160

LEAR.   You nimble lightnings, dart your blinding flames
Into her scornful eyes! Infect her beauty,
You fen-suck'd fogs, drawn by the pow'rful sun,
To fall and blast her pride!

REG.   O the blest gods! so will you wish on me   165
When the rash mood is on.

LEAR.   No, Regan, thou shalt never have my curse.
Thy tender-hefted nature shall not give
Thee o'er to harshness. Her eyes are fierce; but thine
Do comfort, and not burn. 'Tis not in thee   170
To grudge my pleasures, to cut off my train,
To bandy hasty words, to scant my sizes,
And, in conclusion, to oppose the bolt
Against my coming in. Thou better know'st
The offices of nature, bond of childhood,   175
Effects of courtesy, dues of gratitude.
Thy half o' th' kingdom hast thou not forgot,
Wherein I thee endow'd.

REG.   Good sir, to th' purpose.

Tucket within.

LEAR.   Who put my man i' th' stocks?

CORN.   What trumpet 's that?

REG.   I know't — my sister's. This approves her letter,   180
That she would soon be here.

---

159 *ingrateful top* ungrateful head. *her young bones* The context makes it certain that this applies to Goneril's own youthful frame. "To breed young bones" is, to be sure, an old phrase for "to be with child," but that does not justify the strange interpretation ("Strike her unborn child") which has found favour with some critics [K].   160 *taking* infectious.   163 *fen-suck'd* drawn up from the swamps.   164 *blast her pride* Q¹; F¹: "blister." Some editors read "blister her." 166 *rash* hasty.   168 *tender-hefted* swayed (heaved) by tender emotions. Some editors read "tender-hearted."   172 *bandy* volley back and forth. *sizes* allowances.   173–4 *oppose . . . coming in* lock your doors against me.   175 *offices*

Enter [Oswald *the*] Steward.

Is your lady come?

LEAR.   This is a slave, whose easy-borrowed pride
Dwells in the fickle grace of her he follows.
Out, varlet, from my sight!

CORN.   What means your Grace?

Enter Goneril.

LEAR.   Who stock'd my servant? Regan, I have good hope   185
Thou didst not know on't. — Who comes here? O
heavens!
If you do love old men, if your sweet sway
Allow obedience — if yourselves are old,
Make it your cause! Send down, and take my part!
[*To* Goneril] Art not asham'd to look upon this
beard? —   190
O Regan, wilt thou take her by the hand?

GON.   Why not by th' hand, sir? How have I offended?
All's not offence that indiscretion finds
And dotage terms so.

LEAR.   O sides, you are too tough!
Will you yet hold? How came my man i' th' stocks?   195

CORN.   I set him there, sir; but his own disorders
Deserv'd much less advancement.

LEAR.   You? Did you?

REG.   I pray you, father, being weak, seem so.
If, till the expiration of your month,
You will return and sojourn with my sister,   200

duties. *bond of childhood* obligations of a child toward a parent.   176 *Effects* actions.   178 *purpose* point (of your speech). s.d. *Tucket* series of trumpet notes. *within* behind the scenes.   180 *approves* confirms.   182 *easy-borrowed pride* easily borrowed because it does not take much to make him proud [K].   184 *varlet* fellow. A common term of contempt [K].   187 *sweet sway* benificent rule   188 *Allow* approve of.   193 *indiscretion finds* poor judgment considers.   196 *disorders* misconduct.   197 *much less advancement* far less honour than that [K].   198 *seems so* i.e. be content to speak and act like a feeble old man, and submit without protest to those who have you in charge [K].

Dismissing half your train, come then to me.
I am now from home, and out of that provision
Which shall be needful for your entertainment.

LEAR.   Return to her, and fifty men dismiss'd?   205
No, rather I abjure all roofs, and choose
To wage against the enmity o' th' air,
To be a comrade with the wolf and owl —
Necessity's sharp pinch! Return with her?
Why, the hot-blooded France, that dowerless took
Our youngest born, I could as well be brought   210
To knee his throne, and, squire-like, pension beg
To keep base life afoot. Return with her?
Persuade me rather to be slave and sumpter
To this detested groom.   [*Points at* Oswald.]

GON.   At your choice, sir.

LEAR.   I prithee, daughter, do not make me mad.   215
I will not trouble thee, my child; farewell.
We'll no more meet, no more see one another.
But yet thou art my flesh, my blood, my daughter;
Or rather a disease that's in my flesh,
Which I must needs call mine. Thou art a boil,   220
A plague sore, an embossed carbuncle
In my corrupted blood. But I'll not chide thee;
Let shame come when it will, I do not call it;
I do not bid the Thunder-bearer shoot,
Nor tell tales of thee to high-judging Jove.   225
Mend when thou canst; be better at thy leisure;
I can be patient, I can stay with Regan,
I and my hundred knights.

---

203 *entertainment* proper maintenance; care and attention [K].   206 *To wage against* to wage war with; to meet in a contest of strength [K].   208 *Necessity's sharp pinch* This sums up (as an appositive) what precedes (lines 205–8). It is the hard lot of poverty to be homeless and exposed to cold and storm [K].   209 *hot-blooded* choleric.   211 *knee* kneel before. *squire-like* as if I were one of his attendants [K].   213 *sumpter* packhorse.   214 *detested groom* detestable underling.   221 *embossed* headed; rising in a round knob (like the boss of a shield) [K].   224 *the Thunder-bearer* Jupiter. *shoot* dart his thunderbolts at thee [K].   225 *high-judging Jove* Jove, who judges mankind from his high place in heaven.

REG.   Not altogether so.
 I look'd not for you yet, nor am provided
 For your fit welcome. Give ear, sir, to my sister;   230
 For those that mingle reason with your passion
 Must be content to think you old, and so —
 But she knows what she does.

LEAR.   Is this well spoken?

REG. I dare avouch it, sir. What, fifty followers?
 Is it not well? What should you need of more?   235
 Yea, or so many, sith that both charge and danger
 Speak 'gainst so great a number? How in one house
 Should many people, under two commands,
 Hold amity? 'Tis hard; almost impossible.

GON. Why might not you, my lord, receive attendance   240
 From those that she calls servants, or from mine?

REG. Why not, my lord? If then they chanc'd to slack ye,
 We could control them. If you will come to me
 (For now I spy a danger), I entreat you
 To bring but five-and-twenty. To no more   245
 Will I give place or notice.

LEAR. I gave you all —

REG.   And in good time you gave it!

LEAR. Made you my guardians, my depositaries;
 But kept a reservation to be followed
 With such a number. What, must I come to you   250
 With five-and-twenty, Regan? Said you so?

REG. And speak't again, my lord. No more with me.

---

226 *Mend* improve. 231 *mingle reason with your passion* consider your violent words and actions in the light of reason and can tell you what such conduct means [K]. 232 *old* She breaks off abruptly, with a gesture: "You are old — and no further explanation is necessary" [K]. 234 *avouch* swear by. 236 *sith that* since. *charge* expense. 242 *slack* neglect. 243 *control* regulate. 246 *notice* recognition. 247 *And in . . . gave it* A characteristic interruption by the soft-spoken but venomous Regan [K]. 248 *Made you my guardians* entrusted all my possessions to your care [K]. *depositaries* synonymous with "guardians" [K].

LEAR.   Those wicked creatures yet do look well-favour'd
          When others are more wicked; not being the worst
          Stands in some rank of praise. [*To* Goneril] I'll go with
              thee.   255
          Thy fifty yet doth double five-and-twenty,
          And thou art twice her love.

GON.   Hear me, my lord.
          What need you five-and-twenty, ten, or five,
          To follow in a house where twice so many
          Have a command to tend you?

REG.   What need one?   260

LEAR.   O, reason not the need! Our basest beggars
          Are in the poorest thing superfluous.
          Allow not nature more than nature needs,
          Man's life is cheap as beast's. Thou art a lady:
          If only to go warm were gorgeous,   265
          Why, nature needs not what thou gorgeous wear'st,
          Which scarcely keeps thee warm. But, for true need —
          You heavens, give me that patience, patience I need!
          You see me here, you gods, a poor old man,
          As full of grief as age; wretched in both.   270
          If it be you that stirs these daughters' hearts
          Against their father, fool me not so much
          To bear it tamely; touch me with noble anger,
          And let not women's weapons, water drops,
          Stain my man's cheeks! No, you unnatural hags!   275
          I will have such revenges on you both
          That all the world shall — I will do such things —

---

253 *Those wicked creatures* The demonstrative "those" has no personal applica-
tion. Lear's remark is a general truth: "Such creatures as are wicked always have
a good appearance in contrast with others that are more wicked" [ᴋ]. *well-
favour'd* fair, handsome.   259 *To follow* to be your followers.   261–8 *O reason
not . . . I need* Lear distinguishes between absolute necessity (in which sense his
daughters have used the word "need") and that which may be properly regarded
as necessary for comfort and dignity. But he breaks off abruptly when about to
define "true need" (line 267); for the thought forces itself upon him that the
one thing he really "needs" is the gift of "patience" (i.e. fortitude), which may
keep him from the shame of tears [ᴋ].   261–2 *Our basest . . . superfluous* the
most miserable beggars have some things among their poorest possessions that
they do not actually need — that they could get along without [ᴋ].   265–6 *If*

What they are yet, I know not; but they shall be
The terrors of the earth! You think I'll weep.
No, I'll not weep.   280
I have full cause of weeping, but this heart
Shall break into a hundred thousand flaws
Or ere I'll weep. O fool, I shall go mad!

>   *Exeunt* Lear, Gloucester, Kent, *and*
>   Fool.

>   *Storm and tempest.*

CORN.   Let us withdraw; 'twill be a storm.

REG.   This house is little; the old man and 's people   285
        Cannot be well bestow'd.

GON.   'Tis his own blame; hath put himself from rest
        And must needs taste his folly.

REG.   For his particular, I'll receive him gladly,
        But not one follower.

GON.   So am I purpos'd.   290
        Where is my Lord of Gloucester?

CORN.   Followed the old man forth.

>   *Enter* Gloucester.

>   He is return'd.

GLOU.   The King is in high rage.

CORN.   Whither is he going?

GLOU.   He calls to horse, but will I know not whither.

---

only . . . *gorgeous wear'st* if mere warmth were all the gorgeousness that a lady
required of her apparel, then the gorgeousness of your attire would not be needed,
for gorgeousness is certainly not — like warmth — a natural necessity [K].   268
that patience . . . need that degree of fortitude (strength to endure suffering)
that my case requires — it is fortitude that I need [K]   272 *fool me not so much*
do not make me so much of a weakling [K].   279 *terrors of the earth* things so
terrible as to affright the whole world [K].   282 *flaws* fragments.   283 *Or ere*
before.   286 *bestow'd* accommodated.   288 *taste his folly* suffer the consequences
of his folly [K].   289 *For his particular* in so far as he personally is concerned —
excluding his followers.   290 *purpos'd* determined.   293-4 *Whither . . . horse*
F¹; not in Q¹.

CORN.   'Tis best to give him way; he leads himself.   295

GON.   My lord, entreat him by no means to stay.

GLOU.   Alack, the night comes on, and the bleak winds
Do sorely ruffle. For many miles about
There's scarce a bush.

REG.   O, sir, to wilful men
The injuries that they themselves procure   300
Must be their schoolmasters. Shut up your doors.
He is attended with a desperate train,
And what they may incense him to, being apt
To have his ear abus'd, wisdom bids fear.

CORN.   Shut up your doors, my lord; 'tis a wild night.   305
My Regan counsels well. Come out o' th' storm.

Exeunt.

---

295 *to give him way* not to hinder his departure [K].   *he leads himself* he sub-
mits to no guidance; he insists on having his own way [K].   297 *bleak* Q¹; F¹:
"high."   298 *ruffle* rage. A strong word. A "ruffler" is a brawling ruffian [K].   302
a desperate train Regan, like Goneril, shamelessly misrepresents the character of
Lear's knights [K].   303 *incense* instigate.   *apt* ready. Much more active than in
modern usage [K].   304 *abus'd* deceived.

Act Three

$\Diamond$

SCENE I. [*A heath.*]

Storm still. Enter Kent *and a* Gentleman *at several
doors.*

KENT. Who's there, besides foul weather?

GENT. One minded like the weather, most unquietly.

KENT. I know you. Where's the King?

GENT. Contending with the fretful elements;
Bids the wind blow the earth into the sea,   5
Or swell the curled waters 'bove the main,
That things might change or cease; tears his white hair,
Which the impetuous blasts, with eyeless rage,
Catch in their fury and make nothing of;
Strives in his little world of man to outscorn   10
The to-and-fro-conflicting wind and rain.
This night, wherein the cub-drawn bear would couch,
The lion and the belly-pinched wolf

III.I. 2 *minded . . . unquietly* in a disturbed state of mind.   6 *curled waters*
waves. *main* land.   7–15 *tears his . . take all* Q¹; not in F¹.   8 *eyeless* blind —
since they rage at everything without discrimination or definite object [K].   9
make nothing of show no respect for [K].   10 *his little world of man* A man is a
microcosm ("a little cosmos," "a universe in miniature") in comparison with the
macrocosm, "the great cosmos" [K]. The analogy of the human body to the physical earth, each being composed of the four elements of earth, air, fire, and water,
is a Renaissance commonplace.   11 *to-and-fro conflicting* moving in all directions
in angry conflict.   12 *cub-drawn* sucked dry by her cubs, and thus ravenous and
fierce. *couch* lie hidden from the storm [K].   13 *belly-pinched* starved.

Keep their fur dry, unbonneted he runs,
And bids what will take all.

KENT.   But who is with him?   15

GENT.   None but the fool, who labours to outjest
His heart-struck injuries.

KENT.   Sir, I do know you,
And dare upon the warrant of my note
Commend a dear thing to you. There is division
(Although as yet the face of it be cover'd   20
With mutual cunning) 'twixt Albany and Cornwall;
Who have (as who have not, that their great stars
Thron'd and set high?) servants, who seem no less,
Which are to France the spies and speculations
Intelligent of our state. What hath been seen,   25
Either in snuffs and packings of the Dukes,
Or the hard rein which both of them have borne
Against the old kind King, or something deeper,
Whereof, perchance, these are but furnishings —
But, true it is, from France there comes a power   30
Into this scattered kingdom, who already,
Wise in our negligence, have secret feet
In some of our best ports and are at point
To show their open banner. Now to you:
If on my credit you dare build so far   35
To make your speed to Dover, you shall find
Some that will thank you, making just report
Of how unnatural and bemadding sorrow
The King hath cause to plain.

---

15 *bids . . . take all* "Take all!" is the cry of the gambler when he stakes, at a final cast of the dice, all the money that he has left. Hence it is used figuratively as a cry of despair or desperate defiance [K]   16 *to outjest* to relieve by his jests. It is the Fool's tragedy that his efforts to cheer up his master serve only to emphasize Lear's folly and its dreadful results; for the Fool's mind instinctively concentrates on that one idea and he calls Lear "fool" over and over again [K]. 18 *warrant of my note* assurance of my knowledge of you.   19 *Commend* entrust. *dear thing* important matter.   22–9 *Who have . . . furnishings* F¹; not in Q¹.   23 *no less* nothing more or less than servants.   24 *speculations* spies.   25 *What hath been seen* what has been already discernible [K].   26 *snuffs* cases in which they have openly taken offence at each other's actions [K].   *packings* intrigues, secret plots.   29 *furnishings* pretexts that conceal the real purpose of the

        I am a gentleman of blood and breeding,   40
        And from some knowledge and assurance offer
        This office to you.

GENT.   I will talk further with you.

KENT.   No, do not.
        For confirmation that I am much more
        Than my out-wall, open this purse and take   45
        What it contains. If you shall see Cordelia
        (As fear not but you shall), show her this ring,
        And she will tell you who your fellow is
        That yet you do not know. Fie on this storm!
        I will go seek the King.   50

GENT.   Give me your hand. Have you no more to say?

KENT.   Few words, but, to effect, more than all yet:
        That, when we have found the King (in which your
           pain
        That way, I'll this), he that first lights on him
        Holla the other.   *Exeunt [severally].*   55

     ◇◇◇◇◇◇◇◇◇◇◇◇◇◇◇◇◇

        SCENE II. *[Another part of the heath.]*

        Storm still. Enter Lear *and* Fool.

LEAR.   Blow, winds, and crack your cheeks! rage! blow!
        You cataracts and hurricanoes, spout

French invasion [K]. 30–42 *But, true . . . to you* Q¹; not in F¹.   30 *power* army.
31 *scattered* divided.   32 *Wise in* taking advantage of.   *have secret feet* have
secretly set foot.   33 *at point* fully prepared.   35 *my credit* your trust in me.
37 *making* if you make.   *just* true and accurate.   39 *plain* complain.   41 *assur-*
ance trustworthy information.   42 *office* duty.   45 *out-wall* exterior appearance
(Kent is wearing a servant's clothes).   48 *your fellow* your companion; your
associate in the King's service. Thus Kent confirms the suggestion that he is a
more important person than his present position would indicate [K].   52 *to effect*
in importance.   53–4 *in which . . . this* in which task (pain) you go that way
while I go this way.
     III.II. 2 *cataracts* the floodgates of heaven.   *hurricanoes* water-spouts. Lear is
calling for another Deluge to destroy the earth.

Till you have drench'd our steeples, drown'd the cocks!
You sulph'rous and thought-executing fires,
Vaunt-couriers to oak-cleaving thunderbolts,   5
Singe my white head! And thou, all-shaking thunder,
Strike flat the thick rotundity o' th' world,
Crack Nature's moulds, all germains spill at once,
That make ingrateful man!

FOOL. O nuncle, court holy water in a dry house is better than   10
this rain water out o' door. Good nuncle, in, and ask thy
daughters blessing! Here's a night pities neither wise
men nor fools.

LEAR. Rumble thy bellyful! Spit, fire! spout, rain!
Nor rain, wind, thunder, fire are my daughters.   15
I tax not you, you elements, with unkindness.
I never gave you kingdom, call'd you children,
You owe me no subscription. Then let fall
Your horrible pleasure. Here I stand your slave,
A poor, infirm, weak, and despis'd old man.   20
But yet I call you servile ministers,
That will with two pernicious daughters join
Your high-engender'd battles 'gainst a head
So old and white as this! O! O! 'tis foul!

FOOL. He that has a house to put 's head in has a good head-   25
piece.

> The codpiece that will house
> Before the head has any,
> The head and he shall louse:

---

3 *drown'd* submerged.   *cocks* weathercocks.   4 *thought-executing fires* lightning
flashes as swift as thought.   5 *Vaunt-couriers* forerunners, heralds.   *thunderbolts*
Fiery bolts, or stone missiles, were supposed to be discharged from the clouds by
the thunder [K].   8 *Nature's moulds* the moulds which Nature uses in forming
men [K].   *germains* the seeds from which all matter springs. Lear is calling for
the end of human reproduction.   *spill* destroy.   10 *court holy-water* A slang expression for "flattering speech."   16 *tax not you* do not accuse you.   18 *subscription* deference, obedience.   21 *ministers* agents.   23 *high-engender'd* en-
gendered high in the heavens. There is also a suggestion of the meaning "sub-
lime" [K].   *battles* battalions, armies.   25–6 *good headpiece* The Fool puns on
two senses of the phrase: (a) a good helmet, covering for the head, and (b) a good
head — i.e. a wise brain [K].   27–30 *The codpiece . . . marry many* the man
who begets children before he has a house will surely become a lousy vagabond.

So beggars marry many.   30
The man that makes his toe
What he his heart should make
Shall of a corn cry woe,
And turn his sleep to wake.

For there was never yet fair woman but she made   35
mouths in a glass.

Enter Kent.

LEAR.   No, I will be the pattern of all patience; I will say
nothing.

KENT.   Who's there?

FOOL.   Marry, here's grace and a codpiece; that's a wise man   40
and a fool.

KENT.   Alas, sir, are you here? Things that love night
Love not such nights as these. The wrathful skies
Gallow the very wanderers of the dark
And make them keep their caves. Since I was man,   45
Such sheets of fire, such bursts of horrid thunder,
Such groans of roaring wind and rain, I never
Remember to have heard. Man's nature cannot carry
Th' affliction nor the fear.

LEAR.   Let the great gods,
That keep this dreadful pudder o'er our heads,   50
Find out their enemies now. Tremble, thou wretch,
That hast within thee undivulged crimes
Unwhipp'd of justice. Hide thee, thou bloody hand;

Thus it is that many beggars get married [K].   31-4 *The man . . . wake* the
man who exchanges the places of his toe and his heart will get a corn on his
heart instead of on his foot, and that will give him a heartache as will keep him
awake nights. The Fool alludes to Lear's folly in showing favour to Goneril and
Regan and disowning Cordelia [K].   35-6 *made . . . glass* practised making pretty
faces in a mirror [K].   44 *Gallow* terrify. A very strong word. Whalemen still
used "gallied" to describe a whale that is panic-stricken [K]. *wanderers of the
dark* night-prowling wild beasts.   48-9 *cannot carry . . . fear* cannot bear up
under the actual bodily affliction (the buffeting by the storm) and the terror that
accompanies it [K].   50 *pudder* hubbub, turmoil. The same word as "pother"
[K].   51 *Find out* i.e. by the terror which such offenders must show [K].   53
Unwhipp'd of unpunished by.

Thou perjur'd, and thou simular of virtue
That art incestuous. Caitiff, in pieces shake   55
That under covert and convenient seeming
Hast practis'd on man's life. Close pent-up guilts,
Rive your concealing continents, and cry
These dreadful summoners grace. I am a man
More sinn'd against than sinning.

KENT.   Alack, bareheaded?   60
Gracious my lord, hard by here is a hovel;
Some friendship will it lend you 'gainst the tempest.
Repose you there, whilst I to this hard house
(More harder than the stones whereof 'tis rais'd,
Which even but now, demanding after you,   65
Denied me to come in) return, and force
Their scanted courtesy.

LEAR.   My wits begin to turn.
Come on, my boy. How dost, my boy? Art cold?
I am cold myself. Where is this straw, my fellow?
The art of our necessities is strange,   70
That can make vile things precious. Come, your hovel.
Poor fool and knave, I have one part in my heart
That's sorry yet for thee.

FOOL.   [sings]
    He that has and a little tiny wit —
        With hey, ho, the wind and the rain —   75

54 *simular* simulator, counterfeiter (F¹; Q¹, K: "simular man").   55 *Caitiff* wretch.
56 *under covert . . . seeming* under such an appearance of conventional virtue as
masked thy purpose [K].   57 *practis'd on* plotted against.   58-9 *Rive . . . grace*
break open the concealments that hide you, and appeal to these dreadful summoners for mercy. A "summoner" is an officer who summons offenders to an ecclesi-
astical court [K].   59 *I* Emphatic. Thus Lear points out his reason for not fear-
ing the storm [K].   62 *lend* afford.   63 *hard* cruel. *house* household (the occu-
pants as well as the building).   65 *demanding after* asking for.   66 *Denied* for-
bade.   67 *scanted courtesy* niggardly hospitality. *My wits begin to turn* The
first intimation of Lear's delirium [K].   70 *art* The figure alludes to alchemy,
which professed to turn base metals into gold and silver [K].   72-3 *Pool fool
. . . for thee* Here for the first time Lear expresses real concern and kindness for
his fellow man.   76 *Must . . . fit* must make his happiness fit his fortunes; must
be contented and happy, even when his fortunes are bad [K]   77 *Though the* F¹;
Q¹, K: "For the."   78 *True* Lear accepts the Fool's saying as applicable to him-

> Must make content with his fortunes fit,
> Though the rain it raineth every day.

LEAR.   True, my good boy. Come, bring us to this hovel.

Exeunt [Lear *and* Kent].

FOOL.   This is a brave night to cool a courtesan. I'll speak a
prophecy ere I go: 80
>   When priests are more in word than matter;
>   When brewers mar their malt with water;
>   When nobles are their tailors' tutors,
>   No heretics burn'd, but wenches' suitors;
>   When every case in law is right,   85
>   No squire in debt nor no poor knight;
>   When slanders do not live in tongues,
>   Nor cutpurses come not to throngs;
>   When usurers tell their gold i' th' field,
>   And bawds and whores do churches build: 90
>   Then shall the realm of **Albion**
>   Come to great confusion.
>   Then comes the time, who lives to see't,
>   That going shall be us'd with feet.

This prophecy Merlin shall make, for I live before his   95
time.   *Exit.*

---

self [K].   *my good* Q¹; not in F¹.   79–96 *This is . . . his time* F¹; not in Q¹. Most
critics regard the passage as in interpolation. The verses are a parody of an old
epigram entitled "Merlin's Prophecy." The original (well known in Shakespeare's
time) was commonly, though absurdly, ascribed to Chaucer [K].   79 *brave* fine.
81 *more in word than manner* better in talk than in substance; or better in
preaching than in practice [K].   83 *their tailors' tutors* even greater experts in
clothing than the tailors they employ [K].   88 *cutpurses* literally, thieves who
slash purses (worn as a pouch at the girdle) and steal the contents; then, in general, pickpockets [K].   89 *tell* count.   92 *confusion* a ruinous condition [K].   93
who if anybody.   94 *That going . . . feet* when feet shall be used for walking.
An intentionally absurd truism — such as fools frequently pronounced with a
solemn air as a burlesque on the philosophers' profound adages. The audience is
at liberty to make it mean: "The world shall once more be in a normal condition"
[K].   95–6 *This . . . time* This line makes the Fool a real prophet, for Merlin's
date was centuries later than Lear's. He is the seer of Arthurian legend [K].

◇◇◇◇◇◇◇◇◇◇◇◇◇◇◇◇◇

SCENE III. [Gloucester's *Castle*.]

Enter Gloucester *and* Edmund.

GLOU.   Alack, alack, Edmund, I like not this unnatural dealing!
When I desir'd their leave that I might pity him, they
took from me the use of mine own house, charg'd me
on pain of perpetual displeasure neither to speak of
him, entreat for him, nor any way sustain him.   5

EDM.   Most savage and unnatural!

GLOU.   Go to; say you nothing. There is division betwixt the
Dukes, and a worse matter than that. I have received a
letter this night — 'tis dangerous to be spoken — I have
lock'd the letter in my closet. These injuries the King   10
now bears will be revenged home; there's part of a
power already footed; we must incline to the King. I
will seek him and privily relieve him. Go you and maintain talk with the Duke, that my charity be not of him
perceived. If he ask for me, I am ill and gone to bed.   15
Though I die for't, as no less is threat'ned me, the King
my old master must be relieved. There is some strange
thing toward, Edmund. Pray you be careful.   *Exit.*

EDM.   This courtesy, forbid thee, shall the Duke
Instantly know, and of that letter too.   20
This seems a fair deserving, and must draw me
That which my father loses — no less than all.
The younger rises when the old doth fall.   *Exit.*

III.III. 5 *nor any way sustain him* nor do anything whatever to relieve him [K].
7 *division* strife, contention.   8 *worse* more serious.   10 *closet* private room.   11
home to the utmost.   12 *power* army.   *footed* landed.   *incline to* take the part of.
13 *seek* Q¹; F¹: "look."   *privily* secretly.   18 *toward* in preparation, coming.   19
forbid forbidden.   21 *This seems . . . deserving* my giving the Duke this information will seem to him a good piece of service [K].

◇◇◇◇◇◇◇◇◇◇◇◇◇◇◇◇◇

SCENE IV. [*The heath. Before a hovel.*]

Storm still. Enter Lear, Kent, *and* Fool.

KENT.   Here is the place, my lord. Good my lord, enter.
The tyranny of the open night 's too rough
For nature to endure.

LEAR.   Let me alone.

KENT.   Good my lord, enter here.

LEAR.   Wilt break my heart?

KENT.   I had rather break mine own. Good my lord, enter.   5

LEAR.   Thou think'st 'tis much that this contentious storm
Invades us to the skin. So 'tis to thee;
But where the greater malady is fix'd,
The lesser is scarce felt. Thou'dst shun a bear;
But if thy flight lay toward the roaring sea,   10
Thou'dst meet the bear i' th' mouth. When the mind 's
        free,
The body 's delicate. The tempest in my mind
Doth from my senses take all feeling else
Save what beats there. Filial ingratitude!
Is it not as this mouth should tear this hand   15
For lifting food to't? But I will punish home!
No, I will weep no more. In such a night
To shut me out! Pour on; I will endure.
In such a night as this! O Regan, Goneril!
Your old kind father, whose frank heart gave all!   20
O, that way madness lies; let me shun that!
No more of that.

III.iv. 2 *tyranny of the open night* boisterous roughness of such a night in the open air [K].   3 *nature* a man's natural strength [K].   10 *roaring* F¹; Q¹, K: "raging."   11 *free* untroubled, at peace.   12 *delicate* sensitive to pain.   14 *beats there* throbs in my mind and heart. "There" is emphatic [K].   15 *as* as if.   16 *home* to the utmost.   17–18 *In such . . . endure* F¹; not in Q¹.   20 *frank* generous.

KENT.	Good my lord, enter here.
LEAR.	Prithee go in thyself; seek thine own ease.
	This tempest will not give me leave to ponder
	On things would hurt me more. But I'll go in. 25
	[*To the* Fool] In, boy; go first. — You houseless poverty —
	Nay, get thee in. I'll pray, and then I'll sleep.

Exit [Fool].

	Poor naked wretches, wheresoe'er you are,
	That bide the pelting of this pitiless storm,
	How shall your houseless heads and unfed sides, 30
	Your loop'd and window'd raggedness, defend you
	From seasons such as these? O, I have ta'en
	Too little care of this! Take physic, pomp;
	Expose thyself to feel what wretches feel,
	That thou mayst shake the superflux to them 35
	And show the heavens more just.
EDG.	[*within*] Fathom and half, fathom and half! Poor Tom!

Enter Fool [*from the hovel*].

FOOL.	Come not in here, nuncle, here's a spirit. Help me, help me!
KENT.	Give me thy hand. Who's there? 40
FOOL.	A spirit, a spirit! He says his name's poor Tom.
KENT.	What art thou that dost grumble there i' th' straw? Come forth.

Enter Edgar [*disguised as a madman*].

26–7 *In . . . sleep* F¹; not in Q¹.   26 *houseless poverty* unsheltered pauper (the abstract used for the concrete).   29 *bide* suffer, endure.   31 *loop'd and window'd* Synonymous: "full of holes." A "loop" is, literally, a "loophole" [K].   33 *Take physic, pomp* O ye great and mighty ones of the earth, take this remedy to cure your unfeeling hearts [K].   35–6 *That thou . . . more just* that you may cast off what you do not need ("the superflux," superfluity) and bestow it on them, and so may make God's treatment of humanity more impartial than it now seems to be. Precisely the same lesson is expressed by Gloucester in IV.1.65–71 [K].   37 *Fathom . . . Poor Tom* Edgar speaks as if he were a sailor sounding the depth of the water in the hold of a leaking ship. He is almost "swamped" by the storm [K] (F¹; not in Q¹).   44–5 *Through . . . cold wind* A line from a popular ballad of the time (Q¹; F¹: "blow the winds").   45 *thy bed* F¹; Q¹, K: "thy cold bed."   47 *Didst thou give* F¹; Q¹, K: "Hast thou giuen".   *daughters* F¹; Q¹, K: "two daugh-

EDG.   Away! the foul fiend follows me! Through the sharp
        hawthorn blows the cold wind. Humh! go to thy bed,   45
        and warm thee.

LEAR.   Didst thou give all to thy daughters, and art thou come
        to this?

EDG.   Who gives anything to poor Tom? whom the foul fiend
        hath led through fire and through flame, through ford   50
        and whirlpool, o'er bog and quagmire; that hath laid
        knives under his pillow and halters in his pew, set rats-
        bane by his porridge, made him proud of heart, to ride
        on a bay trotting horse over four-inch'd bridges, to
        course his own shadow for a traitor. Bless thy five wits!   55
        Tom's acold. O, do de, do de, do de. Bless thee from
        whirlwinds, star-blasting, and taking! Do poor Tom
        some charity, whom the foul fiend vexes. There could I
        have him now — and there — and there again — and
        there!   *Storm still.*   60

LEAR.   What, have his daughters brought him to this pass?
        Couldst thou save nothing? Would'st thou give 'em all?

FOOL.   Nay, he reserv'd a blanket, else we had been all sham'd.

LEAR.   Now all the plagues that in the pendulous air
        Hang fated o'er men's faults light on thy daughters!   65

KENT.   He hath no daughters, sir.

LEAR.   Death, traitor! nothing could have subdu'd nature
        To such a lowness but his unkind daughters.
        Is it the fashion that discarded fathers

---

ters."   49 *Who gives* Edgar, taking his cue from Lear's word "give," repeats the
kind of petition expected of Bedlam beggars, who "enforce charity" with "prayers" as well as "with lunatic bans" (II.iii.19–20) [K].   51–3 *laid knives . . . por-
ridge* That demons might tempt a man to commit suicide was a common idea of
the time.   52 *pew* a gallery in a house or outside a chamber window — not, a
pew in church [K].   55 *course* chase. *five wits* These were common wit, imagination, fantasy, estimation, and memory — the five mental powers of man.   56 *O, do
. . . do de* He is shuddering with cold [K].   57 *star-blasting* being destroyed by
the power of malignant stars. *taking* infection; the stroke of disease [K].   58–60
There could . . . and there Edgar makes grabs at different parts of his body as if
to catch vermin — or devils [K].   61 *What, have his* THEOBALD; F¹: "Ha's his"; Q¹:
"What, his."   62 *Would'st* F¹; Q¹, K: "Didst."   64 *pendulous* overhanging.   67
subdu'd reduced. *nature* a man's natural powers.

	Should have thus little mercy on their flesh? 70
	Judicious punishment! 'Twas this flesh begot
	Those pelican daughters.
EDG.	Pillicock sat on Pillicock's Hill. 'Allow, 'allow, loo, loo!
FOOL.	This cold night will turn us all to fools and madmen.
EDG.	Take heed o' th' foul fiend; obey thy parents; keep thy 75
	word justly; swear not; commit not with man's sworn
	spouse; set not thy sweet heart on proud array. Tom 's
	acold.
LEAR.	What hast thou been?
EDG.	A servingman, proud in heart and mind; that curl'd 80
	my hair, wore gloves in my cap; serv'd the lust of my
	mistress' heart and did the act of darkness with her;
	swore as many oaths as I spake words, and broke them
	in the sweet face of heaven; one that slept in the con-
	triving of lust, and wak'd to do it. Wine lov'd I deeply, 85
	dice dearly; and in woman out-paramour'd the Turk.
	False of heart, light of ear, bloody of hand; hog in sloth,
	fox in stealth, wolf in greediness, dog in madness, lion
	in prey. Let not the creaking of shoes nor the rustling
	of silks betray thy poor heart to woman. Keep thy foot 90
	out of brothel, thy hand out of placket, thy pen from
	lender's book, and defy the foul fiend. Still through the

---

70 *thus little . . . flesh* Edgar has gone so far in his impersonation of a Bedlam beggar as to pierce his arms with splinters or thorns [K].   71 *Judicious* well judged, just and fitting, condign [K].   72 *pelican* The young of the pelican were believed to feed upon the blood of their mother.   73 *Pillicock* Edgar in pre-tended madness, echoes Lear's word "pelican," distorting it to "Pillicock" (a term of comic endearment) and reciting part of a nursery rhyme [K].   *'Allow . . . loo* a wild "halloo," as if he were calling a hawk [K].   75 *obey thy parents* Edgar speaks solemnly as if he were trying to recite the Ten Commandments [K].   76 *word justly* POPE; F¹: "words Iustice"; Q¹: "words iustly."   81 *wore gloves in my cap* To wear a lady's glove in the cap was a common attention on the part of a gallant [K].   85 *deeply* Q¹; F¹: "deerely."   86 *out-paramour'd* surpassed in the number of my mistresses [K].   *the Turk* the Great Turk, the Sultan.   87 *light of ear* ready to listen to evil reports, slander, flattery.   87–9 *hog in sloth . . . lion in prey* The Seven Deadly Sins were figured in the shape of seven animals [K].   89–90 *Let not . . . woman* do not give your heart to a woman as soon as you hear her shoes creak and her silk gown rustle. Shoes that creaked were fashionable [K]   91 *placket* the slit in a petticoat.   92 *lender's book* The borrower was ex-pected to sign an acknowledgment of receipt in the moneylender's book of

hawthorn blows the cold wind; says suum, mun, hey, no,
nonny. Dolphin my boy, boy, sessa! let him trot by.

Storm still.

LEAR.   Thou wert better in a grave than to answer with thy   95
uncover'd body this extremity of the skies. Is man no
more than this? Consider him well. Thou ow'st the
worm no silk, the beast no hide, the sheep no wool, the
cat no perfume. Ha! Here's three on's are sophisticated!
Thou art the thing itself; unaccommodated man is no   100
more but such a poor, bare, forked animal as thou art.
Off, off, you lendings! Come, unbutton here.

[Tears at his clothes.]

FOOL.   Prithee, nuncle, be contented! 'Tis a naughty night to
swim in. Now a little fire in a wild field were like an old
lecher's heart — a small spark, all the rest on's body cold.   105
Look, here comes a walking fire.

Enter Gloucester *with a torch.*

EDG.   This is the foul Flibbertigibbet. He begins at curfew,
and walks till the first cock. He gives the web and the
pin, squints the eye, and makes the harelip; mildews the
white wheat, and hurts the poor creature of earth.   110
Saint Withold footed thrice the 'old;

record [K].   93-4 *suum . . . nonny* He imitates the whistling of the wind [K].
hey no nonny K; F¹: "nonny"; Q¹: "hay no on ny."   94 *my boy, boy* F¹; Q¹, K:
"my boy, my boy."   95 *Thou wert* F¹; Q¹, K: "Why, thou wert." *a grave* F¹; Q¹, K:
"thy grave."   98-9 *the cat* civet cat.   100 *unaccommodated man* pure and
simple — the thing itself — without any of the artificial furnishings to which he is
accustomed [K].   101 *forked* two-legged.   102 *Off, off* To tear off one's clothes
is a common symptom of delirium [K]. *lendings* Clothes are not given to man by
nature: they are "lent" him by art [K]. *unbutton* Lear instinctively uses the imperative, for he has never before taken off his clothes without a valet's services
[K].   103 *naughty* very bad, wicked; not a trivial or childish word, as in modern
usage [K].   107 *foul* F¹; Q¹, K: "foul fiend." *Flibbertigibbet* a dancing devil. *curfew* nine P.M.   108 *till the* Q¹; F¹: "at." *first cock* midnight.   108-9 *the web
and the pin* An old name for the disease of the eye known as "cataract" [K].   109
harelip cleft upper lip.   111 *Saint Withold* a famous English exorcist of evil
spirits. Edgar is reciting a charm. To tell how St. Withold encountered and sub-
dued the demon and her offspring served as a charm against her power (F¹:
"Swithold," a popular corruption). *footed* traversed. *the 'old* the wold — an
upland plain.

        He met the nightmare, and her nine fold;
           Bid her alight
           And her troth plight,
        And aroint thee, witch, aroint thee!   115

KENT.   How fares your Grace?

LEAR.   What's he?

KENT.   Who's there? What is't you seek?

GLOU.   What are you there? Your names?

EDG.   Poor Tom, that eats the swimming frog, the toad, the 120
todpole, the wall-newt and the water; that in the fury
of his heart, when the foul fiend rages, eats cow-dung
for sallets, swallows the old rat and the ditch-dog, drinks
the green mantle of the standing pool; who is whipp'd
from tithing to tithing, and stock-punish'd and impris- 125
on'd; who hath had three suits to his back, six shirts to
his body, horse to ride, and weapon to wear;
        But mice and rats, and such small deer,
          Have been Tom's food for seven long year.
Beware my follower. Peace, Smulkin! peace, thou fiend! 130

GLOU.   What, hath your Grace no better company?

EDG.   The prince of darkness is a gentleman!
Modo he's call'd, and Mahu.

GLOU.   Our flesh and blood is grown so vile, my lord,
That it doth hate what gets it.   135

---

114 *her troth plight* pledge her solemn word (not to do any harm) [K]. 115 *And aroint thee* Addressed by the reciter directly to the demon: "Away with thee"; "be gone" [K]. 121 *todpole* tadpole. *wall-newt* wall-lizard. *water* water-newt. 123 *sallets* salads. *ditch-dog* dead dog thrown into a ditch. 124 *mantle* scum. *standing* stagnant. 125 *tithing* district within a parish; it contained ten families. A statute of 1597 provided for the whipping of vagabonds from parish to parish until they reached their own, if it could be determined. *stock-punish'd* Q^1;F^1: "stockt, punish'd." 126 *hath had* Q^1; F^1: "hath." *three suits* the regular wardrobe of a male servant. 128 *deer* game. 130 *Smulkin* one of the devils described in Harsnet's DECLARATION, as creeping out of a man's ear in the form of a mouse. 132 *The prince . . . gentleman* and therefore good enough company even for a king [K]. 133 *Modo* a devil described by Harsnet as a great general in hell. *Mahu* another devil described by Harsnet as "generall Dictator of hell." 135 *gets* begets. 137 *suffer* permit. 143 *philosopher* man of science. "Philosophy"

EDG.   Poor Tom 's acold.

GLOU. Go in with me. My duty cannot suffer
       T' obey in all your daughters' hard commands.
       Though their injunction be to bar my doors
       And let this tyrannous night take hold upon you,   140
       Yet have I ventur'd to come seek you out
       And bring you where both fire and food is ready.

LEAR. First let me talk with this philosopher.
       What is the cause of thunder?

KENT. Good my lord, take his offer; go into th' house.   145

LEAR. I'll talk a word with this same learned Theban.
       What is your study?

EDG.   How to prevent the fiend and to kill vermin.

LEAR. Let me ask you one word in private.

KENT. Importune him once more to go, my lord.   150
       His wits begin t' unsettle.

GLOU.   Canst thou blame him?

                                              Storm still.

       His daughters seek his death. Ah, that good Kent!
       He said it would be thus — poor banish'd man!
       Thou say'st the King grows mad: I'll tell thee, friend,
       I am almost mad myself. I had a son,   155
       Now outlaw'd from my blood. He sought my life

---

was the regular word for what we call "science" [K]. Edgar's naked appearance
might have recalled that of the philosopher Diogenes in John Lyly's play
CAMPASPE. Lear in what follows appears to be taking Edgar for the traditional
court philosopher and asking him such questions as these court functionaries
were called upon to answer.   144 *What . . . thunder* A much-discussed scientific
problem in old times [K].   146 *Theban* Why Lear should associate Thebes with
science has never been explained.   147 *What is your study* what is your special
department of scientific research? Edgar picks up the word "study" and applies it
in another sense: "That to which I give all my attention is — how to forestall the
assaults of the fiend and kill the vermin that torment me" [K].   149 *in private*
Lear speaks as if the learned philosopher had answered him sensibly, and as if,
therefore, a private conference with him might be useful in the present crisis [K].
156 *outlaw'd from my blood* deprived of his position as my child.

But lately, very late. I lov'd him, friend —
No father his son dearer. True to tell thee,
The grief hath craz'd my wits. What a night 's this!
I do beseech your Grace —

LEAR.   O, cry you mercy, sir.   160
Noble philosopher, your company.

EDG.   Tom's acold.

GLOU.   In, fellow, there, into th' hovel; keep thee warm.

LEAR.   Come, let's in all.

KENT.   This way, my lord.

LEAR.   With him!
I will keep still with my philosopher.   165

KENT.   Good my lord, soothe him; let him take the fellow.

GLOU.   Take him you on.

KENT.   Sirrah, come on; go along with us.

LEAR.   Come, good Athenian.

GLOU.   No words, no words! hush.   170

EDG.   Child Rowland to the dark tower came;
His word was still
            Fie, foh, and fum!
            I smell the blood of a British man.

                                    Exeunt.

159 *craz'd* The literal meaning is "cracked" [K].   160 *cry you mercy* I beg your
pardon for not attending to you. Lear is a little impatient at being interrupted
in his conference with the "noble philosopher" [K].   166 *soothe him* indulge
him; let him have his own way. To "soothe" is literally to "reply 'Sooth' " (i.e.
"True!") to whatever a person says [K].   169 *Athenian* Since Athenians were
considered more learned and civilized than Thebans, Lear's estimate of his "philosopher" seems to be improving.   171 *Child Rowland . . . came* This may or
may not be a line from some ballad — now lost beyond recovery. "Child" was the
old title for a candidate for knighthood, not yet dubbed "Sir Knight" [K].
Rowland Roland, Charlemagne's nephew and the chief Knight in the Charlemagne
epic cycle [K].   172 *His word was still* his motto or watchword always was.

III.v. 1 *I will have my revenge* Edmund has informed Cornwall of Gloucester's
intention to relieve Lear and to join the invading party in the King's interest
(III.III.7*ff*) [K].   2 *censured* judged — not blamed [K].   3 *something fears me*

◇◇◇◇◇◇◇◇◇◇◇◇◇◇◇◇

SCENE V. [Gloucester's *Castle.*]

Enter Cornwall *and* Edmund.

CORN.   I will have my revenge ere I depart his house.

EDM.   How, my lord, I may be censured, that nature thus gives
          way to loyalty, something fears me to think of.

CORN.   I now perceive it was not altogether your brother's evil
          disposition made him seek his death; but a provoking   5
          merit, set awork by a reproveable badness in himself.

EDM.   How malicious is my fortune that I must repent to be
          just! This is the letter he spoke of, which approves him
          an intelligent party to the advantages of France. O
          heavens! that this treason were not — or not I the de-   10
          tector!

CORN.   Go with me to the Duchess.

EDM.   If the matter of this paper be certain, you have mighty
          business in hand.

CORN.   True or false, it hath made thee Earl of Gloucester.   15
          Seek out where thy father is, that he may be ready for
          our apprehension.

---

frightens me somewhat.   4–6 *I now perceive . . . in himself* I had supposed
that it was merely your brother's evil disposition that made him seek your
father's death. I now perceive that there was something else that impelled him —
namely the fact that your father deserved to die. That fact, however, needed
your brother's evil nature to make it operate as a cause for his murderous plot
[K].   5–6 *a provoking merit* i.e. on Gloucester's part. "Merit" means "deserts" —
a deserving (of death). Cornwall regards Gloucester as a traitor, and therefore as a
complete villain. His character, he suggests, might tempt anyone to kill him.
"Provoking" means "inciting" [K].   6 *in himself* in Edgar.   8 *just* righteous, upright. Loyalty, Edmund implies, has forced him to reveal his father's treason.
approves proves.   9 *an intelligent . . . France* a person engaged in giving information that will aid the invading King of France. "Intelligent" has the active
sense: "giving information" [K].   17 *apprehension* arrest.

EDM.   [*aside*] If I find him comforting the King, it will stuff
his suspicion more fully. — I will persever in my course
of loyalty, though the conflict be sore between that and   20
my blood.

CORN.   I will lay trust upon thee, and thou shalt find a dearer
father in my love.   *Exeunt.*

◇◇◇◇◇◇◇◇◇◇◇◇◇◇◇◇◇

SCENE VI.
[*A farmhouse near* Gloucester's *Castle.*]

Enter Gloucester, Lear, Kent, Fool, *and* Edgar.

GLOU.   Here is better than the open air; take it thankfully. I
will piece out the comfort with what addition I can. I
will not be long from you.

KENT.   All the power of his wits have given way to his impatience. The gods reward your kindness!   5

                                        Exit [Gloucester].

EDG.   Frateretto calls me, and tells me Nero is an angler in
the lake of darkness. Pray, innocent, and beware the
foul fiend.

FOOL.   Prithee, nuncle, tell me whether a madman be a gentleman or a yeoman.   10

---

18 *comforting* aiding.   21 *my blood* my natural feelings toward my kindred [K].
III.VI. 4 *have* Attracted into the plural by the intervening "wits" [K]. *impatience*
passion, lack of self-control. 6 *Frateretto* a devil mentioned in Harsnet's DECLARA-
TION. *Nero* In Rabelais it is the Emperor Trajan who is doomed to fish (for frogs)
in hell forever, whereas Nero is doomed to play his fiddle there, as he supposedly
had done while Rome burned.   7 *innocent* fool.   9–10 *Prithee . . . yeoman*
The fool expects no answer to his conundrum and of course rejects Lear's passionate solution and furnishes the "correct" answer, which involves a wittily il-
logical inference from a bit of more or less proverbial worldly wisdom. Then he
continues his discourse on madmen with a further definition: "He's mad that
trusts," etc. [K].   *yeoman* one who holds property but is not a gentleman in rank
[K].   12–14 *No . . . him* F¹; not in Q¹.   16 *hizzing* A form of "hissing." It suggests the whizzing sound of the red-hot weapons as they are to be brandished by the
thousand assailants [K].   17–54 *The foul fiend . . . her scape* Q¹; not in F¹.   20

LEAR. A king, a king!

FOOL. No, he's a yeoman that has a gentleman to his son; for
he's a mad yeoman that sees his son a gentleman before
him.

LEAR. To have a thousand with red burning spits   15
Come hizzing in upon 'em —

EDG. The foul fiend bites my back.

FOOL. He's mad that trusts in the tameness of a wolf, a horse's
health, a boy's love, or a whore's oath.

LEAR. It shall be done; I will arraign them straight.   20
[*To* Edgar] Come, sit thou here, most learned justicer.
[*To the* Fool] Thou, sapient sir, sit here. Now, you she-
foxes!

EDG. Look, where he stands and glares!
Want'st thou eyes at trial, madam?
        Come o'er the bourn, Bessy, to me.   25

FOOL.   Her boat hath a leak,
               And she must not speak
        Why she dares not come over to thee.

EDG. The foul fiend haunts poor Tom in the voice of a nightingale. Hoppedance cries in Tom's belly for two white   30
herring. Croak not, black angel; I have no food for thee.

KENT. How do you, sir? Stand you not so amaz'd.

---

arraign them In his delirium Lear abandons the idea of attacking his daughters
with an armed force and decides to bring them to trial [K].   21 *justicer* judge.
24 *Want'st . . . madam* Edgar addresses the imaginary Goneril or Regan whom
Lear is arraigning: "Do you wish for spectators at your trial, madam? If so,
there's a fiend to glare at you" [K].   25 *Come . . . to me* Edgar, with a beckoning
gesture, addresses the imaginary Goneril or Regan in the words of an old song
in which a lover calls upon his sweetheart to come to him "across the brook"
[K]. *bourn* brook (CAPELL; Q¹: "broome").   29 *voice of a nightingale* The Fool
has sung the three lines that precede, which are his improvisation, not a part of
the old song [K].   30 *Hoppedance* a devil in Harsnet's DECLARATION. *cries in
Tom's belly* He refers to the rumbling sound that indicates an empty stomach
[K]. *white* unsmoked (as opposed to the "black angel" — smoked devil).   32
amaz'd in a maze. A very strong word indicating a state of utter confusion [K].

Will you lie down and rest upon the cushions?

LEAR.   I'll see their trial first. Bring in their evidence.
[*To* Edgar] Thou, robed man of justice, take thy place.   35
[*To the* Fool] And thou, his yokefellow of equity,
Bench by his side. [*To* Kent] You are o' th' commission,
Sit you too.

EDG.   Let us deal justly.
           Sleepest or wakest thou, jolly shepherd?   40
               Thy sheep be in the corn;
           And for one blast of thy minikin mouth
               Thy sheep shall take no harm.
Purr! the cat is gray.

LEAR.   Arraign her first. 'Tis Goneril. I here take my oath be-   45
fore this honourable assembly, she kick'd the poor King
her father.

FOOL.   Come hither, mistress. Is your name Goneril?

LEAR.   She cannot deny it.

FOOL.   Cry you mercy, I took you for a joint-stool.   50

LEAR.   And here's another, whose warp'd looks proclaim
What store her heart is made on. Stop her there!
Arms, arms! sword! fire! Corruption in the place!
False justicer, why hast thou let her scape?

EDG.   Bless thy five wits!   55

---

34 *their evidence* the witnesses who are to testify against them [K].   35 *robed* Edgar
wears a blanket which Lear takes for a justice's robe of office [K] (POPE; Q¹: "robbed").
37 *Bench* take thy seat on the bench as a judge [K].   *o' th' commission* commissioned a judge.   41 *corn* wheatfield.   42 *one blast* the time it takes to play
one strain on your shepherd's pipe [K].   *minikin* delicate, little.   44 *cat is gray*
Devils often took the form of gray cats.   50 *Cry . . . stool* A conventional jocose
apology for overlooking a person. The Fool takes professional delight in this opportunity to give the worn-out phrase a point; for, in this case, the stool is there
and Goneril is not. A "joint-stool" is a stool fitted together by a joiner (a furni-
ture maker) in distinction from one of ruder manufacture [K].   51 *warp'd* perverse, unnatural.   52 *store* material. *Stop her there* In his delirium Lear sees
Regan escaping from the courtroom [K].   53 *Corruption in the place* bribery in

KENT.   O pity! Sir, where is the patience now
        That you so oft have boasted to retain?

EDG.   [*aside*] My tears begin to take his part so much
        They'll mar my counterfeiting.

LEAR.   The little dogs and all,   60
        Tray, Blanch, and Sweetheart, see, they bark at me.

EDG.   Tom will throw his head at them. Avaunt, you curs!
                Be thy mouth or black or white,
                Tooth that poisons if it bite;
                Mastiff, greyhound, mongrel grim,   65
                Hound or spaniel, brach or lym,
                Bobtail tyke or trundle-tail —
                Tom will make him weep and wail;
                For, with throwing thus my head,
                Dogs leap the hatch, and all are fled.   70
        Do de, de, de. Sessa! Come, march to wakes and fairs
        and market towns. Poor Tom, thy horn is dry.

LEAR.   Then let them anatomize Regan. See what breeds about
        her heart. Is there any cause in nature that makes these
        hard hearts? [*To* Edgar] You, sir — I entertain you for   75
        one of my hundred; only I do not like the fashion of
        your garments. You'll say they are Persian; but let them
        be chang'd.

KENT.   Now, good my lord, lie here and rest awhile.

LEAR.   Make no noise, make no noise; draw the curtains. So, so,   80
        so. We'll go to supper i' th' morning.

---

the seat of justice [K].   56 *patience* self-control.   66 *lym* lymner, a kind of
bloodhound (HANMER; F¹: "Hym"; Q¹: "him").   67 *tyke* cur (Q¹; F¹: "tight").
trundle-tail a dog with a long drooping tail which he seems to "trundle" or drag
along after him [K].   68 *him* F¹; Q¹, K: "them."   70 *leap* Q¹; F¹: "leapt." *hatch*
lower half of a two-part or "Dutch" door.   71 *wakes* parish feasts.   71–2 *fairs
. . . towns* In such places a beggar is likely to fare well.   72 *Poor Tom . . .
dry* A Poor Tom formula in begging for drink [K]. Tom o' Bedlams wore large
horns about their necks for this purpose. Edgar is suggesting also that he is too
exhausted to maintain his role as Poor Tom.   73 *anatomize* dissect.   75 *entertain* engage.   77 *Persian* Persian costumes were proverbially gorgeous (F¹; Q¹, K:
"Persian attire").   80 *curtains* of an imaginary bed.   81 *morning* F¹; Q¹, K: "morning, so, so, so."

FOOL.   And I'll go to bed at noon.

Enter Gloucester.

GLOU.   Come hither, friend. Where is the King my master?

KENT.   Here, sir; but trouble him not; his wits are gone.

GLOU.   Good friend, I prithee take him in thy arms.   85
        I have o'erheard a plot of death upon him.
        There is a litter ready; lay him in't
        And drive towards Dover, friend, where thou shalt meet
        Both welcome and protection. Take up thy master.
        If thou shouldst dally half an hour, his life,   90
        With thine, and all that offer to defend him,
        Stand in assured loss. Take up, take up!
        And follow me, that will to some provision
        Give thee quick conduct.

KENT.   Oppressed nature sleeps.
        This rest might yet have balm'd thy broken sinews.   95
        Which, if convenience will not allow,
        Stand in hard cure. [*To the* Fool] Come, help to bear
            thy master.
        Thou must not stay behind.

GLOU.   Come, come, away!

                            Exeunt [*all but* Edgar].

EDG.   When we our betters see bearing our woes,
        We scarcely think our miseries our foes.   100
        Who alone suffers suffers most i' th' mind,
        Leaving free things and happy shows behind;

---

82 *And I'll . . . at noon* The Fool adds his logic to Lear's remark: if supper is
in the morning, bedtime must be at noon. These are the last words that the Fool
speaks in the play (F¹; not in Q¹).   92 *Stand in assured loss* are in a condition in
which are sure to be lost [K].   93 *provision* means of providing for safety [K].
94–7 *Oppressed nature . . . thy master* Q¹; not in F¹.   95 *Sinews* nerves (F¹;
THEOBALD, K: "senses").   96 *convenience* propitious circumstances.   97 *Stand
in hard cure* are in a condition in which cure is difficult [K].   99–112 *When we
. . . lurk* Q¹; not in F¹.   101 *Who alone . . . mind* suffers in his mind more
than one who has companions in his misery. "Alone" and "most" are the emphatic words. Edgar's reflections are merely an elaboration of the familiar proverb: "Misery loves company" [K].   102 *free* care-free.   *happy shows* happy

But then the mind much sufferance doth o'erskip
When grief hath mates, and bearing fellowship.
How light and portable my pain seems now,   105
When that which makes me bend makes the King bow,
He childed as I fathered! Tom, away!
Mark the high noises, and thyself bewray
When false opinion, whose wrong thoughts defile thee,
In thy just proof repeals and reconciles thee.   110
What will hap more to-night, safe scape the King!
Lurk, lurk.   [*Exit.*]

◇◇◇◇◇◇◇◇◇◇◇◇◇◇◇◇◇

SCENE VII. [Gloucester's *Castle.*]

Enter Cornwall, Regan, Goneril, [Edmund *the*] Bastard,
   and Servants.

CORN.   [*to* Goneril] Post speedily to my lord your husband,
        show him this letter. The army of France is landed. —
        Seek out the traitor Gloucester.

                            [*Exeunt some of the* Servants.]

REG.   Hang him instantly.

GON.   Pluck out his eyes.   5

CORN.   Leave him to my displeasure. Edmund, keep you our
        sister company. The revenges we are bound to take
        upon your traitorous father are not fit for your behold-

---

looks; all appearances of happiness [K].   103 *sufferance* suffering.   *o'erskip*
escape, avoid.   104 *bearing* endurance.   105 *portable* endurable.   108 *Mark
the high noises* give careful attention to the discord among the great and high
[K].   108–10 *thyself bewray . . . reconciles thee* reveal thyself — throw off thy
disguise — when the false opinion that now mistakenly regards thee as a villain,
shall, on proof that thou art guiltless, correct itself, and so shall recall thee to
favour and make peace between thee and thy father [K].   109 *thoughts defile* Q¹;
THEOBALD, K: "thought defiles."   111 *What* whatsoever.   112 *Lurk* remain in hiding.
   III.VII.   7 *are bound* have sworn, are obliged.

ing. Advise the Duke where you are going, to a most
festinate preparation. We are bound to the like. Our   10
posts shall be swift and intelligent betwixt us. Farewell,
dear sister; farewell, my Lord of Gloucester.

Enter [Oswald *the*] Steward.

How now? Where's the King?

OSW.   My Lord of Gloucester hath convey'd him hence.
Some five or six and thirty of his knights,   15
Hot questrists after him, met him at gate;
Who, with some other of the lord's dependants,
Are gone with him towards Dover, where they boast
To have well-armed friends.

CORN.   Get horses for your mistress.

GON.   Farewell, sweet lord, and sister.   20

CORN.   Edmund, farewell.

Exeunt Goneril, [Edmund, *and* Os-
wald].

Go seek the traitor Gloucester,
Pinion him like a thief, bring him before us.

[*Exeunt other* Servants.]

Though well we may not pass upon his life
Without the form of justice, yet our power
Shall do a court'sy to our wrath, which men   25
May blame, but not control.

Enter Gloucester, *brought in by two
or three.*

---

9 *Duke* Albany. *where* to whose palace.   10 *festinate* speedy (F²; Q¹: "festuant";
F¹: "festiuate").   *bound to the like* on our way to the same speedy preparation [K].
10–11 *Our posts* the couriers between us and the Duke of Albany [K].   *intelligent*
giving information; furnished with all necessary news of our warlike movements [K].
12 *Lord of Gloucester* Edmund has now been endowed with his father's estates and
his title.   16 *Hot questrists after him* who had been rapid and eager in their search
for him [K].   23 *pass upon* pass judgment upon.   24 *form* outward appearance.   24–6 *yet our . . . control* yet our power shall act in accordance with
the wrath we feel; and nobody can hinder that action, though some may per-

                                    Who's there? the traitor?

REG.   Ingrateful fox! 'tis he.

CORN.   Bind fast his corky arms.

GLOU.   What means your Graces? Good my friends, consider
            You are my guests. Do me no foul play, friends.   30

CORN.   Bind him, I say.   [Servants *bind him*.]

REG.   Hard, hard. O filthy traitor!

GLOU.   Unmerciful lady as you are, I am none.

CORN.   To this chair bind him. Villain, thou shalt find —

                            [Regan *plucks his beard*.]

GLOU.   By the kind gods, 'tis most ignobly done
            To pluck me by the beard.   35

REG.   So white, and such a traitor!

GLOU.   Naughty lady,
            These hairs which thou dost ravish from my chin
            Will quicken, and accuse thee. I am your host.
            With robber's hands my hospitable favours
            You should not ruffle thus. What will you do?   40

CORN.   Come, sir, what letters had you late from France?

REG.   Be simple-answer'd, for we know the truth.

CORN.   And what confederacy have you with the traitors
            Late footed in the kingdom?

REG.   To whose hands
            You have sent the lunatic king: speak.   45

---

haps find it blameworthy [ĸ].   28 *corky* withered (by old age) [ĸ].   29 *means*
F¹, Q¹; F⁴, ĸ: "mean."   30 *foul play* This phrase was not, as in modern usage,
confined to the sense of "murder." It is, in origin, the antithesis to "fair play,"
and suggests something that is out of accord with law and justice [ĸ].   36 *Naughty*
wicked. A strong adjective in Elizabethan English [ĸ].   38 *quicken* come to life.
39 *hospitable favours* features of your host.   40 *ruffle thus* treat with such
violence.   42 *Be simple-answer'd* give plain, straightforward answers.   44 *Late
footed* recently landed.   45 *you have* F¹, Q¹; Q² ĸ: "haue you."

GLOU.   I have a letter guessingly set down,
      Which came from one that's of a neutral heart,
      And not from one oppos'd.

CORN.   Cunning.

REG.   And false.

CORN.   Where hast thou sent the King?

GLOU.   To Dover.   50

REG.   Wherefore to Dover? Wast thou not charg'd at peril —

CORN.   Wherefore to Dover? Let him answer that.

GLOU.   I am tied to th' stake, and I must stand the course.

REG.   Wherefore to Dover?

GLOU.   Because I would not see thy cruel nails   55
      Pluck out his poor old eyes; nor thy fierce sister
      In his anointed flesh stick boarish fangs.
      The sea, with such a storm as his bare head
      In hell-black night endur'd, would have buoy'd up
      And quench'd the stelled fires.   60
      Yet, poor old heart, he holp the heavens to rain.
      If wolves had at thy gate howl'd that stern time,
      Thou shouldst have said, "Good porter, turn the key."
      All cruels else subscribe. But I shall see
      The winged vengeance overtake such children.   65

CORN.   See't shalt thou never. Fellows, hold the chair.
      Upon these eyes of thine I'll set my foot.

GLOU.   He that will think to live till he be old,
      Give me some help! — O cruel! O ye gods!

---

46 *guessingly set down* written without certain knowledge.   51 *at peril* under penalty (of death).   52 *him answer* F¹; Q¹, K: "him first answer."   53 *tied . . . course* A figure from bear-baiting. The bear was tied to a post and dogs were set on to attack him. A "course" (literally, a "running") was one such attack, lasting until the dogs were called off [K].   54 *Dover* F¹; Q¹, K: "Dover, sir."   57 *anointed* Anointing with holy oil was a part of the ceremony of coronation. Thus a king was a consecrated person, whom it was sacrilege to attack [K].   59 *buoy'd* surged. 60 *stelled fires* fires of the stars.   61 *holp* helped.   62 *howl'd* come howling for shelter [K].   63 *turn the key* to let them enter.   64 *All cruels else* all other cruel creatures.   *subscribe* relent, agree to give up their cruelty (F¹; Q¹, K: "sub-

REG.   One side will mock another. Th' other too!   70

CORN.   If you see vengeance —

1. SERV.   Hold your hand, my lord!
            I have serv'd you ever since I was a child;
            But better service have I never done you
            Than now to bid you hold.

REG.   How now, you dog?

1. SERV.   If you did wear a beard upon your chin,   75
            I'ld shake it on this quarrel.

REG.   What do you mean?

CORN.   My villain!   *Draw and fight.*

1. SERV.   Nay, then, come on, and take the chance of anger.

REG.   Give me thy sword. A peasant stand up thus?

                        *She takes a sword and runs at him
                        behind.*

1. SERV.   O, I am slain! My lord, you have one eye left   80
            To see some mischief on him. O!   *He dies.*

CORN.   Lest it see more, prevent it. Out, vile jelly!
            Where is thy lustre now?

GLOU.   All dark and comfortless! Where's my son Edmund?
            Edmund, enkindle all the sparks of nature   85
            To quit this horrid act.

REG.   Out, treacherous villain!
            Thou call'st on him that hates thee. It was he
            That made the overture of thy treasons to us;

---

scrib'd"). 65 *The winged vengeance* the vengeance of the gods, sweeping down
upon them like a bird of prey [K]. 76 *this quarrel* this cause — i.e. the cause for
which I contend in this case; my defence of the old man [K]. *What do you mean*
K; F¹, Q¹ give the line to First Servant. Some editors give it to Cornwall [K]. 77 *villain*
serf. Used rather as a term of abuse than in the literal sense [K]. 78 *chance of
anger* risk of fighting with with an angry man. 81 *mischief* harm, injury. 82 *prevent it* forestall it; prevent it by anticipatory action [K]. 85 *nature* natural feeling. 86 *quit* repay. *Out* out upon thee! An interjection of cursing [K]. 88
overture disclosure.

Who is too good to pity thee.

GLOU. O my follies! Then Edgar was abus'd.   90
       Kind gods, forgive me that, and prosper him!

REG.   Go thrust him out at gates, and let him smell
       His way to Dover.

                    Exit [*one*] *with* Gloucester.

                    How is't, my lord? How look you?

CORN. I have receiv'd a hurt. Follow me, lady.
       Turn out that eyeless villain. Throw this slave   95
       Upon the dunghill. Regan, I bleed apace.
       Untimely comes this hurt. Give me your arm.

                    Exit [Cornwall, *led by* Regan].

2. SERV. I'll never care what wickedness I do,
          If this man come to good.

3. SERV.   If she live long,
          And in the end meet the old course of death,   100
          Women will all turn monsters.

2. SERV. Let's follow the old Earl, and get the bedlam
          To lead him where he would. His roguish madness
          Allows itself to anything.

3. SERV. Go thou. I'll fetch some flax and whites of eggs   105
          To apply to his bleeding face. Now heaven help him!

                                   Exeunt.

---

90 *abus'd* deceived, wronged.   93 *How look you* how does it look with you; how
are you?   97 *Untimely* since it disables me when I should be leading my army
against the invaders [K].   98–106 *I'll never . . . help him* Q¹; not in F¹.   101
Women will all turn monsters because they will lose all fear of vengeance from the
gods for any misdeed, however flagrant [K].   102 *the bedlam* the mad beggar —
Edgar.   103–4 *His roguish . . . anything* the fact that he is a vagabond (a rogue)
and a madman makes it possible for him do to anything without being called to
account [K].

IV.I 1 *thus* in this beggarly condition [K].   *contemn'd* despised, held in contempt.   3 *most dejected* most cast down — synonymous with "lowest." Edgar

Act Four

◇◇

SCENE I. [*The heath.*]

Enter Edgar.

EDG.   Yet better thus, and known to be contemn'd,
Than still contemn'd and flatter'd. To be worst,
The lowest and most dejected thing of fortune,
Stands still in esperance, lives not in fear.
The lamentable change is from the best;   5
The worst returns to laughter. Welcome then,
Thou unsubstantial air that I embrace!
The wretch that thou hast blown unto the worst
Owes nothing to thy blasts.

            Enter Gloucester, *led by an* Old Man.

                   But who comes here?
My father, poorly led? World, world, O world!   10
But that thy strange mutations make us hate thee,
Life would not yield to age.

OLD MAN.   O my good lord,
I have been your tenant, and your father's tenant,
These fourscore years.

---

comforts himself with the commonplace reflection that any change from the
worst must be for the better [K].   *of* by, at the hands of.   4 *Stands still in
esperance* is in a condition that always admits of hope [K].   6 *returns to laughter*
marks a change for the better — to a state of happiness.   6–9 *Welcome . . . But*
F¹; not in Q¹.   9 *Owes nothing to thy blasts* and therefore need have no fear of
what they can do to him. The figure is from the relation of creditor and debtor;
when a man's debts are paid, he fears no creditor [K].   10 *poorly led* led by a
poor man — a beggar.   11–12 *But that . . . to age* the only thing that makes us
grow old and die is our hatred of life in this world, and that hatred is caused
by the strange vicissitudes of fortune [K].

GLOU.   Away, get thee away! Good friend, be gone.   15
         Thy comforts can do me no good at all;
         Thee they may hurt.

OLD MAN.   You cannot see your way.

GLOU.   I have no way, and therefore want no eyes;
         I stumbled when I saw. Full oft 'tis seen
         Our means secure us, and our mere defects   20
         Prove our commodities. Ah dear son Edgar,
         The food of thy abused father's wrath!
         Might I but live to see thee in my touch,
         I'ld say I had eyes again!

OLD MAN.   How now? Who's there?

EDG.   [aside] O gods! Who is't can say "I am at the worst"?   25
         I am worse than e'er I was.

OLD MAN.   'Tis poor mad Tom.

EDG.   [aside] And worse I may be yet. The worst is not
         So long as we can say "This is the worst."

OLD MAN. Fellow, where goest?

GLOU.   Is it a beggarman?

OLD MAN. Madman and beggar too.   30

GLOU.   He has some reason, else he could not beg.
         I' th' last night's storm I such a fellow saw,
         Which made me think a man a worm. My son
         Came then into my mind, and yet my mind

---

16 *Thy comforts* thy attempts to aid me in my misery [K].   19 *I stumbled when I saw* when I had my eyes, I walked recklessly and lost my footing. Gloucester refers to the terrible blunder he had made in believing Edmund's lies about Edgar, which, he thinks, ought to have been obvious to any clear-sighted judgment [K].   19–21 *Full oft . . . commodities* Thus Gloucester interprets, "I stumbled when I saw," and applies it as a general truth of common experience: "Prosperity makes us careless, and adversity ("our mere defects") proves to be an advantage, for it forces us to recognize the facts of life." Now, in his blindness, he sees the truth [K].   *secure* makes rash or careless, overconfident.   *defects* lacks, deprivations.   *commodities* advantages, benefits.   22 *The food . . . wrath* that on which his anger fed; the object of his anger [K]   *abused* deceived, betrayed.   23–4 *Might I . . . again* to hold thee in my embrace once more would be as great a blessing as the restoration of eyesight [K].   27–8 *The worst is not . . . worst* for so long as we can take comfort in assuring ourselves that we are at the worst, that comforting reflection shows that we are not hopeless and so not actually at the

Was then scarce friends with him. I have heard more
    since.   35
As flies to wanton boys are we to th' gods.
They kill us for their sport.

EDG.   [*aside*] How should this be?
Bad is the trade that must play fool to sorrow,
Ang'ring itself and others. — Bless thee, master!

GLOU.   Is that the naked fellow?

OLD MAN.   Ay, my lord.   40

GLOU.   Then prithee get thee gone. If for my sake
Thou wilt o'ertake us hence a mile or twain
I' th' way toward Dover, do it for ancient love;
And bring some covering for this naked soul,
Who I'll entreat to lead me.

OLD MAN.   Alack, sir, he is mad!   45

GLOU.   'Tis the time's plague when madmen lead the blind.
Do as I bid thee, or rather do thy pleasure.
Above the rest, be gone.

OLD MAN. I'll bring him the best 'parel that I have,
Come on't what will.   *Exit.* 50

GLOU.   Sirrah naked fellow —

EDG.   Poor Tom's acold. [*Aside*] I cannot daub it further.

GLOU.   Come hither, fellow.

EDG.   [*aside*] And yet I must. — Bless thy sweet eyes, they bleed.

---

worst [K].   33 *a worm* A probable echo of JOB, XXV, 6: "How much less man, that
is a worm? and the son of man, which is a worm?"   34 *Came then into my mind*
because I thought that my son was doubtless a homeless wanderer like that poor
beggar [K].   35 *friends* friendly, kindly disposed.   36 *wanton* playful, irresponsible.
38 *play fool to sorrow* act the fool (as I must do) to one who is in sorrow (as my
father is) [K].   39 *Ang'ring* offending.   41 *Then . . . gone* Q¹; F¹: "Get thee away."
43 *ancient love* old-fashioned love, such as formerly bound the servant to his master.
Gloucester in his despair sees such love as banished from the world.   46 *'tis . . .
blind* Gloucester makes a kind of parable out of his own situation: "So it is in
the world. When the leaders of the people are mad and the people themselves
are blind — that is a sad time for humanity" [K].   47 *do thy pleasure* do what
you please. Gloucester remembers that he is in no condition to give an order to
anybody [K].   52 *daub it further* continue my counterfeiting.   54 *And yet I
must* F¹; not in Q¹.

GLOU.   Know'st thou the way to Dover?   55

EDG.   Both stile and gate, horseway and footpath. Poor Tom
hath been scar'd out of his good wits. Bless thee, good
man's son, from the foul fiend! Five fiends have been in
poor Tom at once: of lust, as Obidicut; Hobbididence,
prince of dumbness; Mahu, of stealing; Modo, of murder;   60
Flibbertigibbet, of mopping and mowing, who since
possesses chambermaids and waiting women. So, bless
thee, master!

GLOU.   Here, take this purse, thou whom the heavens' plagues
Have humbled to all strokes. That I am wretched   65
Makes thee the happier. Heavens, deal so still!
Let the superfluous and lust-dieted man,
That slaves your ordinance, that will not see
Because he does not feel, feel your pow'r quickly;
So distribution should undo excess,   70
And each man have enough. Dost thou know Dover?

EDG.   Ay, master.

GLOU.   There is a cliff, whose high and bending head
Looks fearfully in the confined deep.
Bring me but to the very brim of it,   75
And I'll repair the misery thou dost bear
With something rich about me. From that place
I shall no leading need.

EDG.   Give me thy arm.
Poor Tom shall lead thee.   *Exeunt.*

58–63 *Five fiends . . . master* Q¹; not in F¹.   58 *Five fiends* All are described in
Harsnet's DECLARATION.   61 *Flibbertigibbet* POPE; Q¹: "Stiberdigebit." *mopping
and mowing* grimacing and making faces (THEOBALD; Q¹: "Mobing and Making").
61–2 *who since . . . waiting women* since Flibbertigibbet left me, he has possessed
chambermaids and waiting women, who are for ever twisting their faces into strange
shapes in the attempt to put on elegant airs. Cf. III.ii. 35–6. A "flibbertigibbet" is
a "flirt," a "frivolous creature." Hence this is a good name for the demon that
prompts affected airs and graces [K].   65 *humbled to all strokes* brought so low
that thou sufferest every kind of misery [K].   66 *happier* less wretched. *deal so
still* Gloucester calls upon the gods to make his sufferings a common experience of
the great and high when — as in his own case — they have abused their prosperity
[K].   67–71 *Let . . . enough* let the man who has far more than he needs and is
able to gratify every desire feel your power quickly (as I have been made to feel it).

◇◆◇◆◇◆◇◆◇◆◇◆◇◆◇◆◇

SCENE II.
[*Before the* Duke of Albany's *Palace.*]

Enter Goneril *and* [Edmund *the*] Bastard.

GON.   Welcome, my lord. I marvel our mild husband
Not met us on the way.

                              Enter [Oswald *the*] Steward.

                              Now, where's your master?

OSW.   Madam, within, but never man so chang'd.
I told him of the army that was landed:
He smil'd at it. I told him you were coming: 5
His answer was, "The worse." Of Gloucester's treachery
And of the loyal service of his son
When I inform'd him, then he call'd me sot
And told me I had turn'd the wrong side out.
What most he should dislike seems pleasant to him;   10
What like, offensive.

GON.   [*to Edmund*] Then shall you go no further.
It is the cowish terror of his spirit,
That dares not undertake. He'll not feel wrongs
Which tie him to an answer. Our wishes on the way
May prove effects. Back, Edmund, to my brother.   15
Hasten his musters and conduct his pow'rs.

In this way such men will learn to distribute their superfluous wealth among the needy, and no one will be in want. Compare Lear's expression of the same idea in III.IV. 33–6 [K].   *lust-dieted* whose desires are fed to the full.   68 *slaves your ordinance* subordinates and treats with contempt your injunction (the decree of the gods that man share his wealth).   73 *bending* beetling, overhanging.   74 *fearfully* so as to inspire terror in one who looks over the edge [K].   *in* down into.   *confined deep* the Straits of Dover, hemmed in by land on both sides.

     IV.II. 8 *sot* fool.   9 *had turn'd the wrong side out* because I should have said "Edmund's treachery" and "the loyal service of Gloucester" [K].   11 *What like* what he should like.   12 *cowish* cowardly.   13 *undertake* show activity or enterprise in anything [K].   14 *tie* oblige.   *wishes on the way* hopes we discussed as we travelled (that Albany might die).   15 *prove effects* be fulfilled.   16 *pow'rs* troops.

I must change arms at home and give the distaff
Into my husband's hands. This trusty servant
Shall pass between us. Ere long you are like to hear
(If you dare venture in your own behalf)   20
A mistress's command. Wear this.   [*Gives a favour.*]
                                            Spare speech.
Decline your head. This kiss, if it durst speak,
Would stretch thy spirits up into the air.
Conceive, and fare thee well.

EDM.   Yours in the ranks of death!   *Exit.*

GON.   My most dear Gloucester!   25
O, the difference of man and man!
To thee a woman's services are due;
My fool usurps my body.

OSW.   Madame, here comes my lord.
                                            Exit.

                    Enter Albany.

GON.   I have been worth the whistle.

ALB.   O Goneril,
You are not worth the dust which the rude wind   30
Blows in your face! I fear your disposition.
That nature which contemns it origin
Cannot be bordered certain in itself.
She that herself will sliver and disbranch

---

17 *change* exchange; for I must take the sword and give my husband the distaff.
The distaff was a staff used in spinning. It was the regular emblem of wifely in-
dustry, and also (like the broomstick in modern times) a woman's weapon [K].
arms Q¹; F¹: "names."   21 *A mistress's command* a command from one who is
not only your mistress in rank but your lady-love as well [K].   24 *Conceive* (a)
understand (b) let the seed I have planted in your mind come to life.   26 *O . . .
man* F¹; not in Q¹.   28 *My fool* one who should rather be the court fool than
my husband [K].   *usurps* wrongfully possesses (since Edmund possesses her
heart).   29 *worth the whistle* Goneril implies that her husband has been slow
in meeting her: "There has been a time when I was worth whistling for" [K].   31–
50 *I fear . . . the deep* Q¹; not in F¹.   31 *fear* am worried about.   33 *Cannot
be . . . in itself* can have no sure boundaries of conduct in its own character.
There is no enormity that it may not perpetrate [K].   34 *sliver and disbranch*
cut off. The words are synonymous.   35 *material sap* the tree whence she draws
the vital element that constitutes and nourishes her frame [K].   36 *to deadly use*
to destruction — as the dead branches of a tree are of use only as fuel and so
come to naught [K].   39 *Filths . . . themselves* to the filthy all things taste

	From her material sap, perforce must wither	35
	And come to deadly use.	
GON.	No more! The text is foolish.	
ALB.	Wisdom and goodness to the vile seem vile;	
	Filths savour but themselves. What have you done?	
	Tigers, not daughters, what have you perform'd?	40
	A father, and a gracious aged man,	
	Whose reverence even the head-lugg'd bear would lick,	
	Most barbarous, most degenerate, have you madded.	
	Could my good brother suffer you to do it?	
	A man, a prince, by him so benefited!	45
	If that the heavens do not their visible spirits	
	Send quickly down to tame these vile offences,	
	It will come,	
	Humanity must perforce prey on itself,	
	Like monsters of the deep.	
GON.	Milk-liver'd man!	50
	That bear'st a cheek for blows, a head for wrongs;	
	Who hast not in thy brows an eye discerning	
	Thine honour from thy suffering; that not know'st	
	Fools do those villains pity who are punish'd	
	Ere they have done their mischief. Where's thy drum?	55
	France spreads his banners in our noiseless land,	
	With plumed helm thy state begins to threat,	
	Whiles thou, a moral fool, sits still, and cries	

filthy.   42 *Whose reverence . . . lick* to whom even a sulky bear would do hom-
age by licking his hand [K].   *head-lugg'd* tugged along by the head. The slow
lumbering gait of a bear gives one the impression of surly reluctance [K].   44
suffer permit.   46 *visible* Emphatic: "in visible form" [K].   47 *tame* subdue,
put down.   *these vile* JENNENS; Q¹: "this vild."   48–9 *It will come . . . itself*
the inevitable result will follow — all men will become ferocious animals and
devour each other [K].   50 *Milk-liver'd* white-livered. Cowardice was thought to
be caused by lack of blood in the liver [K].   52–3 *an eye discerning . . . suffering* an eye that can discriminate between what one may honourably endure and
what should spur one to noble resentment [K].   53–9 *that not . . . he so* Q¹;
not in F¹.   55 *Ere . . . mischief* before they have committed the crime for which
they are being punished. She is referring probably to the punishment inflicted upon
Lear before he has had an opportunity to commit the crime of joining the French
invaders. Her exact meaning has been much debated.   56 *noiseless* quiet — i.e.
passive and unresisting [K].   57 *state* government.   *to threat* JENNENS; Q¹:
"thereat."   58 *moral* moralizing; i.e. arguing about the rights and wrongs of the
matter instead of opposing the invader [K].   *sits* Q¹; K: "sit'st."   *cries* Q¹; K: "criest."

"Alack, why does he so?"

ALB.   See thyself, devil!
Proper deformity seems not in the fiend   60
So horrid as in woman.

GON.   O vain fool!

ALB.   Thou changed and self-cover'd thing, for shame!
Bemonster not thy feature! Were't my fitness
To let these hands obey my blood,
They are apt enough to dislocate and tear   65
Thy flesh and bones. Howe'er thou art a fiend,
A woman's shape doth shield thee.

GON.   Marry, your manhood mew!

                    Enter a Gentleman.

ALB.   What news?

GENT.   O, my good lord, the Duke of Cornwall's dead,   70
Slain by his servant, going to put out
The other eye of Gloucester.

ALB.   Gloucester's eyes?

GENT.   A servant that he bred, thrill'd with remorse,
Oppos'd against the act, bending his sword
To his great master; who, thereat enrag'd,   75
Flew on him, and amongst them fell'd him dead;
But not without that harmful stroke which since
Hath pluck'd him after.

---

60 *Proper* to a fiend, and therefore not so horrible as it is in a woman.   61
vain silly.   62-8 *Thou changed . . . mew* Q¹; not in F¹.   62 *self-cover'd* Various meanings are possible (a) your real fiendish self covered by the outward
form of a woman (b) your natural womanly self covered by evil (c) your true
self hidden from yourself.   63 *Bemonster . . . feature* do not allow thy form
and features to be thus transformed into those of a monster [K].   *my fitness* fit
for me.   64 *blood* passionate impulse.   65 *apt* ready.   66-7 *Howe'er . . .
shield thee* however much of a fiend thou art, I see that thy shape is that of a
woman; and so thou art safe from my attack [K].   68 *mew* lock up. The mews
were cages in which falcons were kept. Her precise meaning is not clear, although it is obvious that she is being contemptuous.   73 *thrill'd* excited, moved.

ALB.	This shows you are above,
	You justicers, that these our nether crimes
	So speedily can venge! But O poor Gloucester! 80
	Lost he his other eye?
GENT.	Both, both, my lord.
	This letter, madam, craves a speedy answer.
	'Tis from your sister.
GON.	[*aside*] One way I like this well;
	But being widow, and my Gloucester with her,
	May all the building in my fancy pluck 85
	Upon my hateful life. Another way
	The news is not so tart. — I'll read, and answer. *Exit.*
ALB.	Where was his son when they did take his eyes?
GENT.	Come with my lady hither.
ALB.	He is not here.
GENT.	No, my good lord; I met him back again. 90
ALB.	Knows he the wickedness?
GENT.	Ay, my good lord. 'Twas he inform'd against him,
	And quit the house on purpose, that their punishment
	Might have the freer course.
ALB.	Gloucester, I live
	To thank thee for the love thou show'dst the King, 95
	And to revenge thine eyes. Come hither, friend.
	Tell me what more thou know'st. *Exeunt.*

---

remorse pity.   75 *thereat enrag'd* F²; F¹: "threat — enrag'd."   78 *pluck'd* pulled.
79 *justicers* judges (Q¹; F¹: "Iustices").   *nether crimes* crimes committed on earth.
83 *One way I like this well* In one respect Cornwall's death is good news, since
it has removed an obstacle to Goneril's plans. Her hope was to get rid of her
husband, marry Edmund, and seize Regan's half of the kingdom, thus becoming
sole Queen of Britain. See IV.vi. 26*off*; V.i. 59–65; V.iii. 82*ff* [K]. 85–6 *May . . . life*
may pull down the whole structure that I have raised in my imagination and
bury the rest of my life in its ruins — so that my life will be hateful to me [K].
87 *tart* disagreeable.   90 *back again* as he was on his way back to Gloucester's
castle [K].

◇◇◇◇◇◇◇◇◇◇◇◇◇◇◇

[SCENE III. *The French camp near Dover.*]

Enter Kent *and a* Gentleman.

KENT.   Why the King of France is so suddenly gone back know
you no reason?

GENT.   Something he left imperfect in the state, which since
his coming forth is thought of, which imports to the
kingdom so much fear and danger that his personal   5
return was most required and necessary.

KENT.   Who hath he left behind him general?

GENT.   The Marshal of France, Monsieur La Far.

KENT.   Did your letters pierce the Queen to any demonstration
of grief?   10

GENT.   Ay, sir. She took them, read them in my presence,
And now and then an ample tear trill'd down
Her delicate cheek. It seem'd she was a queen
Over her passion, who, most rebel-like,
Sought to be king o'er her.

KENT.   O, then it mov'd her?   15

GENT.   Not to a rage. Patience and sorrow strove
Who should express her goodliest. You have seen
Sunshine and rain at once: her smiles and tears
Were like, a better way. Those happy smilets

IV.III. Q¹. The entire scene is omitted from F¹.   2 *no reason* Q¹; F¹, K: "the reason."   3 *state* administration of the government.   4-5 *which imports . . . danger* which, unless it is attended to, will bring upon the French kingdom so
much panic and danger [K].   9 *pierce* excite, provoke.   11 *sir* THEOBALD; Q¹:
"say."   12 *trill'd* trickled.   14 *passion* emotion, sorrow. *rebel-like* Impulse and
passion or emotion are often figured as rebelling against one's reason or self-
control [K].   16 *rage* a violent outburst of grief — not wrath [K]. *Patience* self-
control. *strove* POPE; Q¹: "streme."   17 *express her goodliest* give her the most
beautiful expression [K].   19 *Were like, a better way* were like sunshine and
rain at once, but after a better fashion — i.e. the comparison does her smiles and
tears injustice; they were more beautiful than mingled sunshine and rain [K].
smilets little smiles.   20 *seem'd* POPE; Q¹: "seeme."   21 *which* who — i.e. the

That play'd on her ripe lip seem'd not to know   20
What guests were in her eyes, which parted thence
As pearls from diamonds dropp'd. In brief,
Sorrow would be a rarity most belov'd,
If all could so become it.

KENT.   Made she no verbal question?

GENT.   Faith, once or twice she heav'd the name of father   25
Pantingly forth, as if it press'd her heart;
Cried "Sisters, sisters! Shame of ladies! Sisters!
Kent! father! sisters! What, i' th' storm? i' th' night?
Let pity not be believ'd!" There she shook
The holy water from her heavenly eyes,   30
And clamour moisten'd. Then away she started
To deal with grief alone.

KENT.   It is the stars,
The stars above us, govern our conditions;
Else one self mate and make could not beget
Such different issues. You spoke not with her since?   35

GENT.   No.

KENT.   Was this before the King return'd?

GENT.   No, since.

KENT.   Well, sir, the poor distressed Lear's i' th' town;
Who sometime, in his better tune, remembers
What we are come about, and by no means   40
Will yield to see his daughter.

---

guests in her eyes, the tears [K].   **22** *pearls from diamonds dropp'd* We should
remember that it is a courtly gentleman who is speaking, and that elegant language was expected of courtiers. Shakespeare often calls tears "pearls" [K].   **24**
If all . . . it if it could be so becoming to all sorrowful people as it is to her.
25 *heav'd* uttered with difficulty.   **29** *believ'd* believed in (as existent in a world
that sees such deeds) [K].   **31** *And clamour moisten'd* and thus she moistened her
lamentation — i.e. followed her cries of sorrow with tears. The gentleman outdoes
himself in this phrase, but the meaning is clear enough [K].   *moisten'd* CAPELL; Q¹:
"moystened her."   **33** *govern our conditions* determine our characters.   **34** *one
self* one and the same.   *and make* and mate, partner (Q¹; Q², K: "and mate").   **39**
in his better tune in a comparatively lucid interval [K].

GENT.	Why, good sir?
KENT.	A sovereign shame so elbows him; his own unkindness,
	That stripp'd her from his benediction, turn'd her
	To foreign casualties, gave her dear rights
	To his dog-hearted daughters — these things sting 45
	His mind so venomously that burning shame
	Detains him from Cordelia.
GENT.	Alack, poor gentleman!
KENT.	Of Albany's and Cornwall's powers you heard not?
GENT.	'Tis so; they are afoot.
KENT.	Well, sir, I'll bring you to our master Lear 50
	And leave you to attend him. Some dear cause
	Will in concealment wrap me up awhile.
	When I am known aright, you shall not grieve
	Lending me this acquaintance. I pray you go
	Along with me. *Exeunt.* 55

◇◇◇◇◇◇◇◇◇◇◇◇◇◇◇◇◇

SCENE [IV. *The French camp.*]

Enter, with Drum and Colours, Cordelia, Doctor, *and*
Soldiers.

COR.	Alack, 'tis he! Why, he was met even now
	As mad as the vex'd sea, singing aloud,
	Crown'd with rank fumiter and furrow weeds,
	With hardocks, hemlock, nettles, cuckoo flow'rs,

---

42 *sovereign* overpowering. *elbows him* stands by his side like a constant attendant
[K].   43 *stripp'd her from his benediction* deprived her of his blessing when they
parted [K]. *turn'd her* turned her out.   44 *casualties* chances.   48 *powers* troops.
49 *afoot* on the march.   51 *dear* important.   53 *grieve* regret.
IV.IV. 3 *fumiter* fumitory — an herb (THEOBALD; F¹: "Fenitar"; Q¹: "femiter").
3 *furrow weeds* weeds that appear after plowing.   4 *hardocks* Variously explained as "hardbacks," "burdocks," or "harlocks," various weeds. *cuckoo flow'rs*
flowers which bloom in the early spring, when the cuckoo builds its nest.
5 *Darnel* tares.   6 *sustaining corn* life-supporting wheat. *century* troop of a
hundred soldiers.   8 *man's wisdom* science.   10 *worth* property, possessions.
12 *Our . . . nature* the foster nurse of our nature; that which fosters and sus-

Darnel, and all the idle weeds that grow 5
In our sustaining corn. A century send forth.
Search every acre in the high-grown field
And bring him to our eye. [*Exit an* Officer.] What can
    man's wisdom
In the restoring his bereaved sense?
He that helps him take all my outward worth. 10

DOCT.   There is means, madam.
Our foster nurse of nature is repose,
The which he lacks. That to provoke in him
Are many simples operative, whose power
Will close the eye of anguish.

COR.   All blest secrets, 15
All you unpublish'd virtues of the earth,
Spring with my tears! be aidant and remediate
In the good man's distress! Seek, seek for him!
Lest his ungovern'd rage dissolve the life
That wants the means to lead it.

Enter Messenger.

MESS.   News, madam. 20
The British pow'rs are marching hitherward.

COR.   'Tis known before. Our preparation stands
In expectation of them. O dear father,
It is thy business that I go about.
Therefore great France 25
My mourning and importun'd tears hath pitied.
No blown ambition doth our arms incite,

---

tains our life [K].   13 *provoke* induce.   14 *simples* medicinal plants — so called
in contradistinction to "compounds" [K].   15 *secrets* In old times every distin-
guished physician claimed the knowledge of "secrets" — special remedies, unknown to the majority. The next line repeats the sense with elaboration of
phrase [K].   16 *unpublish'd* unknown. *virtues* efficacious medicinal plants [K].
of the earth that grow in the earth. Medicine in Shakespeare's day was, for the
most part, botanical medicine [K].   17 *be aidant and remediate* act as aids and
remedies [K].   18 *distress* Q¹; F¹: "desires."   19 *rage* frenzy.   20 *means to lead
it* the power of reason.   22–3 *Our preparation . . . them* our troops stand
ready to meet them [K].   26 *importun'd* importunate (F¹; Q¹, K: "important").
27 *blown* puffed up, swollen.

But love, dear love, and our ag'd father's right.
Soon may I hear and see him!   *Exeunt.*

◇◈◇◈◇◈◇◈◇◈◇◈◇◈◇◈

SCENE V. [Gloucester's *Castle.*]

Enter Regan *and* [Oswald *the*] Steward.

REG.   But are my brother's pow'rs set forth?

OSW.   Ay, madam.

REG.   Himself in person there?

OSW.   Madam, with much ado.
        Your sister is the better soldier.

REG.   Lord Edmund spake not with your lord at home?

OSW.   No, madam.   5

REG.   What might import my sister's letter to him?

OSW.   I know not, lady.

REG.   Faith, he is posted hence on serious matter.
        It was great ignorance, Gloucester's eyes being out,
        To let him live. Where he arrives he moves   10
        All hearts against us. Edmund, I think, is gone,
        In pity of his misery, to dispatch
        His nighted life; moreover, to descry
        The strength o' th' enemy.

OSW.   I must needs after him, madam, with my letter.   15

REG.   Our troops set forth to-morrow. Stay with us.
        The ways are dangerous.

IV.v. 2 *much ado* great effort. Albany has been reluctant to join in the battle.
6 *might import* could signify. *my sister's letter* the letter with which Oswald
was entrusted by Goneril. Regan is justly suspicious as to its contents. See IV.vi.
26*off* [K]. 8 *serious matter* important business. 9 *ignorance* folly, error. 13
nighted blinded. 17 *ways* roads. 20 *Belike* probably. 25 *eliads* œillades, lan-
guishing looks [K]. 26 *of her bosom* in her confidence. 29 *take this note* take

OSW.   I may not, madam.
My lady charg'd my duty in this business.

REG.   Why should she write to Edmund? Might not you
Transport her purposes by word? Belike,   20
Something — I know not what — I'll love thee much —
Let me unseal the letter.

OSW.   Madam, I had rather —

REG.   I know your lady does not love her husband;
I am sure of that; and at her late being here
She gave strange eliads and most speaking looks   25
To noble Edmund. I know you are of her bosom.

OSW.   I, madam?

REG.   I speak in understanding. Y'are! I know't.
Therefore I do advise you take this note.
My lord is dead; Edmund and I have talk'd,   30
And more convenient is he for my hand
Than for your lady's. You may gather more.
If you do find him, pray you give him this;
And when your mistress hears thus much from you,
I pray desire her call her wisdom to her.   35
So farewell.
If you do chance to hear of that blind traitor,
Preferment falls on him that cuts him off.

OSW.   Would I could meet him, madam! I should show
What party I do follow.

REG.   Fare thee well.   *Exeunt.* 40

_____

note of this.   30 *talk'd* come to an understanding.   31 *convenient* fitting.   32
gather more draw a further inference from the hints that I have given you [K].
33 *this* some love token — not a letter, for when Oswald is searched by Edgar, only
the letter from Goneril is found (IV. VI. 254*ff*) [K]. She may mean "this message" or
"this information."   34 *thus much* what I have told you.   38 *Preferment* promo-
tion, advancement.

◇◇◇◇◇◇◇◇◇◇◇◇◇◇◇◇

SCENE [VI. *The country near Dover.*]

Enter Gloucester, *and* Edgar [*like a* Peasant].

GLOU.   When shall I come to th' top of that same hill?

EDG.   You do climb up it now. Look how we labour.

GLOU.   Methinks the ground is even.

EDG.   Horrible steep.
        Hark, do you hear the sea?

GLOU.   No, truly.

EDG.   Why then, your other senses grow imperfect   5
        By your eyes' anguish.

GLOU.   So may it be indeed.
        Methinks thy voice is alter'd, and thou speak'st
        In better phrase and matter than thou didst.

EDG.   Y'are much deceiv'd. In nothing am I chang'd
        But in my garments.

GLOU.   Methinks y'are better spoken.   10

EDG.   Come on, sir; here's the place. Stand still. How fearful
        And dizzy 'tis to cast one's eyes so low!
        The crows and choughs that wing the midway air
        Show scarce so gross as beetles. Halfway down
        Hangs one that gathers sampire — dreadful trade!   15
        Methinks he seems no bigger than his head.
        The fishermen that walk upon the beach

IV.VI. 6 *anguish* physical pain (not "grief"). 8 *In better phrase and matter* Shakespeare marks the change in Edgar's speech by having him speak in blank verse. 13 *choughs* jackdaws. 14 *gross* large. 15 *sampire* samphire, an aromatic herb which was used in meat relishes after pickling in vinegar. It grew on cliffs overlooking the sea and was gathered by men lowered by ropes for the purpose. 17 *walk* Q¹; F¹: "walk'd." 19 *Diminish'd . . . cock* reduced to the size of her cock-boat — a small ship's boat. 21 *unnumb'red* innumerable. *idle* useless. *pebble* Common as a plural [K]. 23–4 *and the deficient . . . headlong* and I, my sight failing me, fall headlong [K]. 27 *leap upright* Being so near the edge of the cliff to leap upright — let alone forward — would land him in the gulf below. 29 *Fairies* There are two superstitious notions about "fairy gold." One is that it merely seems to be gold, and resumes its real nature as rubbish when the

Appear like mice; and yond tall anchoring bark,
Diminish'd to her cock; her cock, a buoy
Almost too small for sight. The murmuring surge   20
That on th' unnumb'red idle pebble chafes
Cannot be heard so high. I'll look no more,
Lest my brain turn, and the deficient sight
Topple down headlong.

GLOU.   Set me where you stand.

EDG.   Give me your hand. You are now within a foot   25
Of th' extreme verge. For all beneath the moon
Would I not leap upright.

GLOU.   Let go my hand.
Here, friend, 's another purse; in it a jewel
Well worth a poor man's taking. Fairies and gods
Prosper it with thee! Go thou further off;   30
Bid me farewell, and let me hear thee going.

EDG.   Now fare ye well, good sir.

GLOU.   With all my heart.

EDG.   [*aside*]. Why I do trifle thus with his despair
Is done to cure it.

GLOU.   O you mighty gods!   *He kneels.*
This world I do renounce, and, in your sights   35
Shake patiently my great affliction off.
If I could bear it longer and not fall
To quarrel with your great opposeless wills,
My snuff and loathed part of nature should

---

finder has stored it away. The other is that hidden treasure is guarded by
fairies and that they make it multiply miraculously in the possession of the dis-
coverer [K].   33-4 *Why I . . . cure it* A very necessary "aside" for the enlighten-
ment of the audience. Edgar is trying a dangerous experiment, for the agitation
may be too great for Gloucester's strength; but the experiment succeeds [K].
37-8 *fall To quarrel with* come to a state of rebellion against. Gloucester implies
that such rebellion would be a greater sin than suicide [K]. *opposeless* irresisti-
ble.   39 *My snuff* The snuff is the burnt piece of wick which dims the light of
a lamp or candle and causes a disagreeable smoke. The meaning here is explained by the phrase that follows [K]. *loathed part of nature* the remnant of
my natural life, which is hateful to me [K].

	Burn itself out. If Edgar live, O, bless him! 40
	Now, fellow, fare thee well.

He falls [forward and swoons].

EDG.   Gone, sir, farewell. —
And yet I know not how conceit may rob
The treasury of life when life itself
Yields to the theft. Had he been where he thought,
By this had thought been past. — Alive or dead?   45
Ho you, sir! friend! Hear you, sir? Speak! —
Thus might he pass indeed. Yet he revives.
What are you, sir?

GLOU.   Away, and let me die.

EDG.   Hadst thou been aught but gossamer, feathers, air,
So many fathom down precipitating,   50
Thou'dst shiver'd like an egg; but thou dost breathe;
Hast heavy substance; bleed'st not; speak'st; art sound.
Ten masts at each make not the altitude
Which thou hast perpendicularly fell.
Thy life's a miracle. Speak yet again.   55

GLOU.   But have I fall'n, or no?

EDG.   From the dread summit of this chalky bourn.
Look up a-height. The shrill-gorg'd lark so far
Cannot be seen or heard. Do but look up.

GLOU.   Alack, I have no eyes!   60
Is wretchedness depriv'd that benefit
To end itself by death? 'Twas yet some comfort

42–4 *how conceit . . . theft* how powerful imagination may be in rifling life's treasury of all its stores (i.e. of vitality) when life itself does not resist such robbery [K].
46 *Ho you, sir* Edgar now plays the part of a man who, walking on the beach
below, has seen Gloucester fall from the cliff [K].   47 *pass* pass away, die.   49
gossamer a floating thread of a spider's web.   50 *precipitating* falling headlong.
53 *at each* one on top of another.   54 *fell* fallen.   57 *summit* ROWE; F¹: "Som-
net"; Q¹: "sommons."   *bourn* boundary.   58 *a-height* on high.   *shrill-gorg'd*
shrill-throated, shrill-voiced.   63 *beguile* deceive, cheat, elude — i.e. by suicide
[K].   71 *whelk'd and wav'd* rising on the surface into wavelike ridges [K].   *en-*

> When misery could beguile the tyrant's rage
> And frustrate his proud will.

EDG.   Give me your arm.
Up — so. How is't? Feel you your legs? You stand.   65

GLOU.   Too well, too well.

EDG.   This is above all strangeness.
Upon the crown o' th' cliff what thing was that
Which parted from you?

GLOU.   A poor unfortunate beggar.

EDG.   As I stood here below, methought his eyes
Were two full moons; he had a thousand noses,   70
Horns whelk'd and wav'd like the enridged sea.
It was some fiend. Therefore, thou happy father,
Think that the clearest gods, who make them honours
Of men's impossibilities, have preserv'd thee.

GLOU.   I do remember now. Henceforth I'll bear   75
Affliction till it do cry out itself
"Enough, enough," and die. That thing you speak of,
I took it for a man. Often 'twould say
"The fiend, the fiend" — he led me to that place.

EDG.   Bear free and patient thoughts.

> *Enter* Lear, *mad,* [*fantastically dressed
> with weeds*].

                    But who comes here?   80
The safer sense will ne'er accommodate
His master thus.

---

ridged Q¹; F¹: "enraged." Edgar is not thinking of huge billows but of the normal appearance of the surface of the ocean [K].   72 *happy father* fortunate old man. Edgar is not revealing his identity.   73 *clearest* most glorious, most pure. 73-4 *who make . . . impossibilities* who win honour by helping men who cannot help themselves [K].   76-7 *till it . . . and die* until it has had enough of the struggle, gives up, and dies — i.e. affliction itself will die before Gloucester does.   80 *free* free from sorrow, cheerful [K].   81-2 *The safer sense . . . thus* a sound mind would never let its possessor dress himself up in this fashion [K].

LEAR.	No, they cannot touch me for coining; I am the King himself.
EDG.	O thou side-piercing sight! 85
LEAR.	Nature's above art in that respect. There's your press money. That fellow handles his bow like a crow-keeper. Draw me a clothier's yard. Look, look, a mouse! Peace, peace; this piece of toasted cheese will do't. There's my gauntlet; I'll prove it on a giant. Bring up the brown 90 bills. O, well flown, bird! i' th' clout, i' th' clout! Hewgh! Give the word.
EDG.	Sweet marjoram.
LEAR.	Pass.
GLOU.	I know that voice. 95
LEAR.	Ha! Goneril with a white beard? They flatter'd me like a dog, and told me I had the white hairs in my beard ere the black ones were there. To say "ay" and "no" to everything I said! "Ay" and "no" too was no good divinity. When the rain came to wet me once, and the 100 wind to make me chatter; when the thunder would not peace at my bidding; there I found 'em, there I smelt 'em out. Go to, they are not men o' their words! They told me I was everything. 'Tis a lie — I am not ague-proof. 105
GLOU.	The trick of that voice I do well remember.

83–92 *No, they cannot . . . the word* Lear has wandered away from Dover (IV.III. 38). In his delirium he sees constables who try to arrest him as a coiner of counterfeit money. The next moment he is a captain engaged in the enlistment of drafted men and in testing the recruits. Suddenly he catches sight of an imaginary mouse. (Compare his delirium about barking dogs in III.VI. 60–1.) Then he is a champion defying all opponents; then a captain once more; then a spectator at an archery contest; then, catching sight of Edgar, he becomes a sentry and challenges him: "Give the word" [K].   83 *coining* Q¹; F¹: "crying."   86 *Nature's . . . respect* A mildly philosophical reflection: "Art is said to improve nature; but that does not hold true in the case of kingship, for a king's authority comes by nature and nothing can abrogate it" [K].   86–7 *press-money* money paid to a man being recruited.   87 *like a crow-keeper* in a clumsy manner, like a farm-boy used to ward off crows.   88 *clothier's yard* The standard English arrow was a cloth-yard in length [K].   90 *prove it* put my cause (signified by the gauntlet)

Is't not the King?

LEAR.   Ay, every inch a king!
When I do stare, see how the subject quakes.
I pardon that man's life. What was thy cause?
Adultery?   110
Thou shalt not die. Die for adultery? No.
The wren goes to't, and the small gilded fly
Does lecher in my sight.
Let copulation thrive; for Gloucester's bastard son
Was kinder to his father than my daughters   115
Got 'tween the lawful sheets.
To't, luxury, pell-mell! for I lack soldiers.
Behold yond simp'ring dame,
Whose face between her forks presageth snow,
That minces virtue, and does shake the head   120
To hear of pleasure's name.
The fitchew nor the soiled horse goes to't
With a more riotous appetite.
Down from the waist they are Centaurs,
Though women all above.   125
But to the girdle do the gods inherit,
Beneath is all the fiend's.
There's hell, there's darkness, there's the sulphurous pit;
burning, scalding, stench, consumption. Fie, fie, fie! pah,
pah! Give me an ounce of civet, good apothecary, to 130
sweeten my imagination. There's money for thee.

---

to the test of combat [K].   90-1 *brown bills* halberds or pikes varnished to
prevent rust.   91 *bird* The arrow is compared to a falcon.   *clout* bull's eye.
92 *word* password.   96 *Goneril . . . beard* He takes Gloucester for Goneril in
disguise.   96-7 *like a dog* fawningly.   97-8 *told me . . . there* when I was a
beardless boy they told me that I was as wise as an old man [K].   *the white* F¹;
Q¹, K: "white."   99-100 *no good divinity* bad theology. The right doctrine is to
let your "ay" mean "ay" and your "no" mean "no" (MATTHEW, V, 37; JAMES, V,
12) [K].   106 *trick* peculiarity.   107 *Is't not the King* Gloucester's question re-
calls Lear to the subject with which he began, that of sovereignty [K].   109
cause offence.   117 *luxury* lechery.   120 *minces virtue* counterfeits virtue by
her mincing airs — her pretence of delicate prudery [K].   122 *fitchew* polecat.
soiled full-fed with grass in the spring [K].   124 *Centaurs* wildly lustful creatures
of Greek mythology, half man and half horse.   126 *inherit* possess, hold sway.
130-1 *to sweeten* Q¹; F¹: "sweeten."

GLOU. O, let me kiss that hand!

LEAR. Let me wipe it first; it smells of mortality.

GLOU. O ruin'd piece of nature! This great world
Shall so wear out to naught. Dost thou know me?   135

LEAR. I remember thine eyes well enough. Dost thou squiny
at me? No, do thy worst, blind Cupid! I'll not love.
Read thou this challenge; mark but the penning of it.

GLOU. Were all thy letters suns, I could not see.

EDG. [*aside*] I would not take this from report. It is,   140
And my heart breaks at it.

LEAR. Read.

GLOU. What, with the case of eyes?

LEAR. O, ho, are you there with me? No eyes in your head,
nor no money in your purse? Your eyes are in a heavy   145
case, your purse in a light. Yet you see how this world
goes.

GLOU. I see it feelingly.

LEAR. What, art mad? A man may see how this world goes
with no eyes. Look with thine ears. See how yond justice   150
rails upon yond simple thief. Hark in thine ear. Change
places and, handy-dandy, which is the justice, which is
the thief? Thou hast seen a farmer's dog bark at a
beggar?

GLOU. Ay, sir.   155

LEAR. And the creature run from the cur? There thou mightst

---

134 *piece of nature* masterpiece of Nature's workmanship [K].   134–5 *This great
. . . to naught* the universe (the macrocosm) will decay, just as this individual
man (the microcosm) decays.   136 *squiny* squint.   139 *all thy* F¹; Q¹, K: "all the."
see F¹; Q¹, K: "see one."   140 *take* believe. *this* the scene he is witnessing.   143
the case the mere sockets.   144 *are you there with me* is that what you are trying to tell me?   145–6 *in a heavy case* in a sad condition (with a pun on "case"
and "heavy") [K].   148 *feelingly* (a) keenly (b) with my sense of feeling —
since I have no eyes.   149 *this world* F¹; Q¹, K: "the world."   151 *simple* ordinary, mere.   152 *handy-dandy* take your choice. A formula used in a children's
game; the child must choose which hand contains the candy or toy.   157 *image*
likeness, figure.   159 *beadle* parish officer whose duty it was to whip vagabonds
and whores.   161 *kind* manner.   162 *The usurer hangs the cozener* Lear im-

behold the great image of authority: a dog's obey'd in
office.
Thou rascal beadle, hold thy bloody hand!
Why dost thou lash that whore? Strip thine own back.   160
Thou hotly lusts to use her in that kind
For which thou whip'st her. The usurer hangs the
cozener.
Through tatter'd clothes small vices do appear;
Robes and furr'd gowns hide all. Plate sin with gold,
And the strong lance of justice hurtless breaks;   165
Arm it in rags, a pygmy's straw does pierce it.
None does offend, none — I say none! I'll able 'em.
Take that of me, my friend, who have the power
To seal th' accuser's lips. Get thee glass eyes
And, like a scurvy politician, seem   170
To see the things thou dost not. Now, now, now, now!
Pull off my boots. Harder, harder! So.

EDG.   O, matter and impertinency mix'd!
        Reason in madness!

LEAR.   If thou wilt weep my fortunes, take my eyes.   175
        I know thee well enough; thy name is Gloucester.
        Thou must be patient. We came crying hither;
        Thou know'st, the first time that we smell the air
        We wawl and cry. I will preach to thee. Mark.

GLOU.   Alack, alack the day!   180

LEAR.   When we are born, we cry that we are come
        To this great stage of fools. This' a good block.

---

plies that justices are often guilty of usury, and thus far greater criminals than
the cozeners (sharpers, petty cheats) whom they sentence to be hanged [K].
163 *small* Q¹; F¹: "great." *appear* show clearly.   164–9 *Plate . . . lips* F¹; not
in Q¹.   164 *Plate sin* clothe sin with armour (THEOBALD; F¹: "Place sinnes").   167
able 'em warrant them, vouch for them.   168 *Take that of me* Lear imagines
that Gloucester is a criminal, and makes a gesture as if he were handing him a
pardon signed and sealed [K].   170 *scurvy* vile.   173 *matter and impertinency*
good sense and incoherent talk [K].   179 *wawl and cry* Synonymous (F¹; Q¹: "wayl
and cry").   182 *a good block* a hat of good fashion. Whether Lear is wearing a
hat or not in the scene has been much debated. He probably pretends to be re-
moving his hat as one about to deliver a sermon.

It were a delicate stratagem to shoe
A troop of horse with felt. I'll put't in proof,
And when I have stol'n upon these son-in-laws,   185
Then kill, kill, kill, kill, kill, kill!

                Enter a Gentleman [*with* Attendants].

GENT.   O, here he is! Lay hand upon him. — Sir,
        Your most dear daughter —

LEAR.   No rescue? What, a prisoner? I am even
        The natural fool of fortune. Use me well;   190
        You shall have ransom. Let me have a surgeon;
        I am cut to th' brains.

GENT.   You shall have anything.

LEAR.   No seconds? All myself?
        Why, this would make a man a man of salt,
        To use his eyes for garden waterpots,   195
        Ay, and laying autumn's dust.

GENT.   Good sir —

LEAR.   I will die bravely, like a smug bridegroom. What!
        I will be jovial. Come, come, I am a king;
        My masters, know you that?

GENT.   You are a royal one, and we obey you.   200

LEAR.   Then there's life in't. Come, an you get it, you shall get
        it by running. Sa, sa, sa, sa!

                Exit running. [Attendants *follow*.]

GENT.   A sight most pitiful in the meanest wretch,

---

183 *delicate stratagem* neat trick.   184 *in proof* to the test.   185 *son-in-laws*
F¹, Q¹; K: "sons-in-law."   190 *natural fool of fortune* one born to be the
playything or dupe of fortune. There may be a quibble on "natural" in
the sense of "idiot."   192 *cut to th' brains* wounded in the head. Lear uses
the term literally (thinking that he has a head wound) and figuratively (since
he is mad).   194 *a man of salt* That tears are salt is a fact which Shakespeare
never forgets [K].   196 *Ay . . . dust* Q¹; not in F¹.   197 *bravely* in fine attire.
"Smug" repeats the idea; it means "spick and span." Lear is thinking of his floral
adornments [K].   201 *life in't* hope in the situation. *Come* F¹; Q¹, K: "Nay."
202 *Sa, sa, sa, sa* an old hunting cry to call a hound or to urge the dogs forward

	Past speaking of in a king! Thou hast one daughter	
	Who redeems nature from the general curse	205
	Which twain have brought her to.	
EDG.	Hail, gentle sir.	
GENT.	Sir, speed you. What's your will?	
EDG.	Do you hear aught, sir, of a battle toward?	
GENT.	Most sure and vulgar. Every one hears that	
	Which can distinguish sound.	
EDG.	But, by your favour,	210
	How near's the other army?	
GENT.	Near and on speedy foot. The main descry	
	Stands on the hourly thought.	
EDG.	I thank you, sir. That's all.	
GENT.	Though that the Queen on special cause is here,	
	Her army is mov'd on.	
EDG.	I thank you, sir.	215

Exit [Gentleman].

GLOU.	You ever-gentle gods, take my breath from me;	
	Let not my worser spirit tempt me again	
	To die before you please!	
EDG.	Well pray you, father.	
GLOU.	Now, good sir, what are you?	
EDG.	A most poor man, made tame to fortune's blows,	220
	Who, by the art of known and feeling sorrows,	
	Am pregnant to good pity. Give me your hand;	

in chase of the hare. It was also in common use as a rallying cry, or as an interjection of challenge and defiance. Here the King challenges his pursuers: "Come
on! come on! Catch me if you can!" And so he runs off the stage, waving his
arm in a defiant gesture [K].   204 *one* Q¹; F¹: "a."   205 *general* universal.   208
toward in preparation.   209 *vulgar* common knowledge.   212–13 *The main descry
. . . thought* the main body of men is expected to be seen at any hour now.   217
worser spirit evil side of my nature.   218 *father* old man.   220 *tame* humbly
submissive.   221 *by the art . . . sorrows* instructed by heart-felt sorrows I have
known.   222 *pregnant to* readily susceptible to.

I'll lead you to some biding.

GLOU.   Hearty thanks.
The bounty and the benison of heaven
To boot, and boot!

Enter [Oswald *the*] *Steward.*

OSW.   A proclaim'd prize! Most happy!   225
That eyeless head of thine was first fram'd flesh
To raise my fortunes. Thou old unhappy traitor,
Briefly thyself remember. The sword is out
That must destroy thee.

GLOU.   Now let thy friendly hand
Put strength enough to't.   [Edgar *interposes.*]

OSW.   Wherefore, bold peasant,   230
Dar'st thou support a publish'd traitor? Hence!
Lest that th' infection of his fortune take
Like hold on thee. Let go his arm.

EDG.   Chill not let go, zir, without vurther 'cagion.

OSW.   Let go, slave, or thou diest!   235

EDG.   Good gentleman, go your gait, and let poor voke pass.
An chud ha' bin zwagger'd out of my life, 'twould not
ha' bin zo long as 'tis by a vortnight. Nay, come not near
th' old man. Keep out, che vore ye, or Ise try whether
your costard or my ballow be the harder. Chill be plain 240
with you.

OSW.   Out, dunghill!   *They fight.*

EDG.   Chill pick your teeth, zir. Come! No matter vor your
foins.   [Oswald *falls.*]

---

223 *biding* resting place, refuge.   224–5 *The bounty . . . and boot* besides giving you my thanks, I pray heaven to favour and bless you, and may that favour
and blessing be your reward [K].   225 *proclaim'd prize* fugitive with a price on
his head. *happy* opportune.   228 *Briefly thyself remember* think of your sins
quickly (so as to reconcile yourself to heaven before death).   229 *friendly*
since I long for death [K].   231 *publish'd* proclaimed.   234 *Chill . . . vurther
'cagion* Edgar assumes the lingo that, from Elizabethan time to the end of the
eighteenth century, served as the stage dialect of rusticity. It accords well enough
with the dialect of Somersetshire, but the dramatists were not finical [K]. *Chill*

OSW.	Slave, thou hast slain me. Villain, take my purse.	245

If ever thou wilt thrive, bury my body,
And give the letters which thou find'st about me
To Edmund Earl of Gloucester. Seek him out
Upon the British party. O, untimely death! Death!

He dies.

EDG. I know thee well. A serviceable villain,   250
As duteous to the vices of thy mistress
As badness would desire.

GLOU.   What, is he dead?

EDG. Sit you down, father; rest you.
Let's see his pockets; the letters that he speaks of
May be my friends. He's dead. I am only sorry   255
He had no other deathsman. Let us see.
Leave, gentle wax; and, manners, blame us not.
To know our enemies' minds, we rip their hearts;
Their papers, is more lawful.   *Reads the letter.*

"Let our reciprocal vows be rememb'red. You have many   260
opportunities to cut him off. If your will want not, time
and place will be fruitfully offer'd. There is nothing
done, if he return the conqueror. Then am I the prisoner, and his bed my jail; from the loathed warmth
whereof deliver me, and supply the place for your lab-   265
our.
"Your (wife, so I would say) affectionate servant,
                                   "GONERIL."

O indistinguish'd space of woman's will!
A plot upon her virtuous husband's life,
And the exchange my brother! Here in the sands   270
Thee I'll rake up, the post unsanctified

I will. *vurther 'cagion* further occasion.   236 *gait* way. *voke* folk.   237 *chud*
I would.   239 *che vore ye* I warn you. *Ise* I shall.   240 *costard* head. *ballow*
cudgel.   244 *foins* sword thrusts.   245 *Villain* serf.   247 *letters* Oswald was
carrying a letter to Edmund from Goneril (IV.II. 18–19; IV.V. 6, 22). "Letters" is
common in the sense of "letter" (Latin "litterae") [K].   249 *British* Q¹; F¹: "English." *party* side.   254 *the letters* F¹; Q¹, K: "these letters."   256 *deathsman* execu-
tioner.   258 *we rip* F¹; Q¹: "wee'd rip"; K: "we'ld rip."   268 *indistinguish'd space*
limitless range. *will* lust.   271 *rake up* bury hastily and without ceremony [K].
post messenger.

Of murderous lechers; and in the mature time
With this ungracious paper strike the sight
Of the death-practis'd Duke. For him 'tis well
That of thy death and business I can tell.   275

GLOU.   The King is mad. How stiff is my vile sense,
That I stand up, and have ingenious feeling
Of my huge sorrows! Better I were distract.
So should my thoughts be sever'd from my griefs,
And woes by wrong imaginations lose   280
The knowledge of themselves.   *A drum afar off.*

EDG.   Give me your hand.
Far off methinks I hear the beaten drum.
Come, father, I'll bestow you with a friend.   *Exeunt.*

◇◇◇◇◇◇◇◇◇◇◇◇◇◇◇◇◇◇

SCENE VII. [*A tent in the French camp.*]

Enter Cordelia, Kent, Doctor, *and* Gentleman.

COR.   O thou good Kent, how shall I live and work
To match thy goodness? My life will be too short
And every measure fail me.

KENT.   To be acknowledg'd, madam, is o'erpaid.
All my reports go with the modest truth;   5
Nor more nor clipp'd, but so.

COR.   Be better suited.
These weeds are memories of those worser hours.
I prithee put them off.

---

272 *in the mature time* when time is ripe.   273 *ungracious* abominable.   274
death-practis'd Duke Duke whose death is plotted.   277 *ingenious feeling* acute
mental consciousness [K].   278 *distract* insane.   280 *wrong imaginations* illusions.
283 *bestow you* provide a refuge for you.

IV.VII 3 *every measure fail me* since thy goodness is unmeasurable.   5 *All
my reports . . . truth* everything that I have told you (about the King and his
sufferings) corresponds exactly with a moderate expression of the facts [K].   6
suited clothed. Kent is still disguised as a servingman [K].   7 *weeds* clothes.
memories reminders.   9 *shortens my made intent* interferes with (shortens) the

KENT.   Pardon, dear madam.
        Yet to be known shortens my made intent.
        My boon I make it that you know me not   10
        Till time and I think meet.

COR.   Then be't so, my good lord. [*To the* Doctor] How does
            the King?

DOCT.   Madam, sleeps still.

COR.   O you kind gods,
        Cure this great breach in his abused nature!   15
        Th' untun'd and jarring senses, O, wind up
        Of this child-changed father!

DOCT.   So please your Majesty
        That we may wake the King? He hath slept long.

COR.   Be govern'd by your knowledge, and proceed
        I' th' sway of your own will. Is he array'd?   20

                    Enter Lear *in a chair carried by* Serv-
                    ants.

GENT.   Ay, madam. In the heaviness of sleep
        We put fresh garments on him.

DOCT.   Be by, good madam, when we do awake him.
        I doubt not of his temperance.

COR.   Very well.   [*Music.*]

DOCT.   Please you draw near. Louder the music there!   25

COR.   O my dear father, restoration hang
        Thy medicine on my lips, and let this kiss
        Repair those violent harms that my two sisters

---

plan I have made.   10 *My boon I make it* I ask it of you as a special favour
[K].   11 *meet* proper.   16 *wind up* put into proper tune — as the strings of a
musical instrument are tightened.   17 *child-changed* The meaning may be
deliberately ambiguous: (a) changed into a child (b) changed — made mad — by
his children.   20 *I' th' sway of* governed by.   *array'd* dressed (in his royal robes).
24 *doubt not* Q¹; F¹: "doubt." *temperance* normal self-control [K].   24-5 *Very
well . . . there* Q¹; not in F¹.   25 *the music* The beneficial effect of music in the
treatment of madness is an ancient theory [K].

Have in thy reverence made!

KENT.   Kind and dear princess!

COR.   Had you not been their father, these white flakes   30
         Had challeng'd pity of them. Was this a face
         To be oppos'd against the warring winds?
         To stand against the deep dread-bolted thunder?
         In the most terrible and nimble stroke
         Of quick cross lightning? to watch — poor perdu! —   35
         With this thin helm? Mine enemy's dog,
         Though he had bit me, should have stood that night
         Against my fire; and wast thou fain, poor father,
         To hovel thee with swine and rogues forlorn,
         In short and musty straw? Alack, alack!   40
         'Tis wonder that thy life and wits at once
         Had not concluded all. — He wakes. Speak to him.

DOCT.   Madam, do you; 'tis fittest.

COR.   How does my royal lord? How fares your Majesty?

LEAR.   You do me wrong to take me out o' th' grave.   45
         Thou art a soul in bliss; but I am bound
         Upon a wheel of fire, that mine own tears
         Do scald like molten lead.

COR.   Sir, do you know me?

LEAR.   You are a spirit, I know. When did you die?

COR.   Still, still, far wide!   50

DOCT.   He's scarce awake. Let him alone awhile.

LEAR.   Where have I been? Where am I? Fair daylight?

---

29 *in thy reverence* in thee, to whom all reverence is due [K].   30 *white flakes*
Lear's white hair hangs down in long straight strands [K].   32 *warring* Q¹; F¹:
"iarring."   33–6 *To stand . . . helm* Q¹; not in F¹.   33 *dread-bolted* with its
terrible thunderbolts.   35 *cross* zigzag. *perdu* a solitary sentinel keeping watch
far away from the main body and therefore in a very dangerous position [K].
36 *this thin helm* his scanty locks [K].   38 *fain* glad.   39 *rogues* vagabonds.
40 *short and musty straw* Long, clean straw would make a good bed. The straw in
the hovel was damp and musty and had been broken up into short lengths by
constant use as bedding [K].   42 *concluded all* come to a complete end [K].   49

I am mightily abus'd. I should e'en die with pity,
To see another thus. I know not what to say.
I will not swear these are my hands. Let's see.   55
I feel this pin prick. Would I were assur'd
Of my condition!

COR.   O, look upon me, sir,
And hold your hands in benediction o'er me.
No, sir, you must not kneel.

LEAR.   Pray, do not mock me.
I am a very foolish fond old man,   60
Fourscore and upward, not an hour more nor less;
And, to deal plainly,
I fear I am not in my perfect mind.
Methinks I should know you, and know this man;
Yet I am doubtful; for I am mainly ignorant   65
What place this is; and all the skill I have
Remembers not these garments; nor I know not
Where I did lodge last night. Do not laugh at me;
For (as I am a man) I think this lady
To be my child Cordelia.

COR.   And so I am! I am!   70

LEAR. Be your tears wet? Yes, faith. I pray weep not.
If you have poison for me, I will drink it.
I know you do not love me; for your sisters
Have, as I do remember, done me wrong.
You have some cause, they have not.

COR.   No cause, no cause.   75

LEAR. Am I in France?

When Q²; F¹, Q¹: "Where." This reading has been much debated.   50 *wide* wide
of the mark, distracted [K].   51 *scarce awake* We should observe that Lear is no
longer delirious. He merely needs a few minutes to adjust himself to the present
situation, for he has no memory of what has happened in the interval. His confusion is well understood by the Doctor [K].   53 *abus'd* deceived, deluded. Lear
cannot trust the evidence of his senses [K].   59 *No, sir* Q¹; not in F¹.   60 *fond*
doting.   61 *not . . . less* F¹; not in Q¹.   65 *mainly* very, absolutely.   66 *skill*
power of mind [K].   71 *Be your tears wet* Lear still fears that he is suffering from
a delusion [K].

KENT.   In your own kingdom, sir.

LEAR.   Do not abuse me.

DOCT.   Be comforted, good madam. The great rage
          You see is kill'd in him; and yet it is danger
          To make him even o'er the time he has lost.   80
          Desire him to go in. Trouble him no more
          Till further settling.

COR.   Will't please your Highness walk?

LEAR.   You must bear with me.
          Pray you now, forget and forgive. I am old and foolish.

                    Exeunt. Manent Kent *and* Gentle-
                    man.

GENT.   Holds it true, sir, that the Duke of Cornwall was so   85
          slain?

KENT.   Most certain, sir.

GENT.   Who is conductor of his people?

KENT.   As 'tis said, the bastard son of Gloucester.

GENT.   They say Edgar, his banish'd son, is with the Earl of 90
          Kent in Germany.

KENT.   Report is changeable. 'Tis time to look about; the
          powers of the kingdom approach apace.

GENT.   The arbitrement is like to be bloody. Fare you well, sir.

                                        [*Exit.*]

KENT.   My point and period will be throughly wrought,   95
          Or well or ill, as this day's battle 's fought.   *Exit.*

---

77 *abuse* deceive.   78 *great rage* violent delirium.   79–80 *and yet . . . has lost*
Q¹; not in F¹.   80 *even o'er* fill up the gap in. The metaphor may be drawn
from the language of commercial bookkeeping. To "even over" means to make
accounts even.   82 *Till further settling* until he was grown calmer.   83 *walk*
withdraw.   85–96 *Holds . . . fought* Q¹; not in F¹.   88 *conductor* leader, general.   93 *powers* armies.   94 *arbitrement* decision. *like* likely.   95-6 *My point
. . . fought* the completion of my lot in life will be worked out, for good or ill,
according as this battle results in victory or defeat [K].   *throughly* thoroughly,
completely.

Act Five

SCENE I. [*The British camp near Dover.*]

Enter, with Drum *and* Colours, Edmund, Regan,
Gentlemen, *and* Soldiers.

EDM. Know of the Duke if his last purpose hold,
         Or whether since he is advis'd by aught
         To change the course. He's full of alteration
         And self-reproving. Bring his constant pleasure.

                              [*Exit an* Officer.]

REG.   Our sister's man is certainly miscarried.   5

EDM.   'Tis to be doubted, madam.

REG.   Now, sweet lord,
         You know the goodness I intend upon you.
         Tell me — but truly — but then speak the truth —
         Do you not love my sister?

EDM.   In honour'd love.

REG.   But have you never found my brother's way   10
         To the forfended place?

EDM.   That thought abuses you.

V.I. 1 *his last purpose* i.e. to join us in the battle against Cordelia's forces [K].
2 *advis'd by aught* instructed by (induced by consideration of) anything [K]. 3
alteration vacillation. 4 *self-reproving* self-reproach. *constant pleasure* firm decision. 5 *sister's man* i.e. Oswald. *miscarried* come to harm. 6 *doubted* feared.
7 *intend upon you* mean to bestow upon you. 9 *honour'd* honourable. 11
forfended forbidden. 11–13 *That thought . . . call hers* Q¹; not in F¹. *abuses*
deceives.

127

REG.   I am doubtful that you have been conjunct
        And bosom'd with her, as far as we call hers.

EDM.   No, by mine honour, madam.

REG.   I never shall endure her. Dear my lord,   15
        Be not familiar with her.

EDM.   Fear me not.
        She and the Duke her husband!

                        Enter, with Drum *and* Colours, Al-
                        bany, Goneril, Soldiers.

GON.   [*aside*] I had rather lose the battle than that sister
        Should loosen him and me.

ALB.   Our very loving sister, well bemet.   20
        Sir, this I hear: the King is come to his daughter,
        With others whom the rigour of our state
        Forc'd to cry out. Where I could not be honest,
        I never yet was valiant. For this business,
        It touches us as France invades our land,   25
        Not bolds the King, with others whom, I fear,
        Most just and heavy causes make oppose.

EDM.   Sir, you speak nobly.

REG.   Why is this reason'd?

GON.   Combine together 'gainst the enemy;
        For these domestic and particular broils   30
        Are not the question here.

ALB.   Let's then determine
        With th' ancient of war on our proceeding.

EDM.   I shall attend you presently at your tent.

---

12 *am doubtful* suspect. *conjunct* united.   13 *bosom'd* intimate (breast to
breast). *as far . . . hers* in the fullest sense of the word; in respect to all that she
has and is [ĸ].   16 *Fear me not* don't distrust me.   18–19 *I had . . . me* Q¹; not
in F¹.   21 *hear* Q¹; F¹: "heard."   22 *state* government.   23 *cry out* protest.   23–8
Where I . . . speak nobly Q¹; not in F¹.   23 *be honest* be honourable; act with a
good conscience [ĸ].   25 *touches* concerns (Q¹; Q², ĸ: "toucheth").   25–7 *as France
. . . make oppose* insofar as the French king is invading Britain, but not insofar
as he is supporting King Lear and others who (as I fear) have just cause to oppose
us. Albany implies that the government of Britain has been tyrannical of late [ĸ].

REG. Sister, you'll go with us?

GON. No.   35

REG. 'Tis most convenient. Pray go with us.

GON. [*aside*] O, ho, I know the riddle. — I will go.

> [*As they are going out,*] *enter* Edgar
> [*disguised*].

EDG. If e'er your Grace had speech with man so poor,
Hear me one word.

ALB.   I'll overtake you. — Speak.

> *Exeunt* [*all but* Albany *and* Edgar].

EDG. Before you fight the battle, ope this letter.   40
If you have victory, let the trumpet sound
For him that brought it. Wretched though I seem,
I can produce a champion that will prove
What is avouched there. If you miscarry,
Your business of the world hath so an end,   45
And machination ceases. Fortune love you!

ALB. Stay till I have read the letter.

EDG.   I was forbid it.
When time shall serve, let but the herald cry,
And I'll appear again.

ALB. Why, fare thee well. I will o'erlook thy paper.   50

> *Exit* [Edgar].

> *Enter* Edmund.

EDM. The enemy 's in view; draw up your powers.

28 *reason'd* being argued.   30 *domestic and particular* family and personal [ĸ].
32 *th' ancient of war* our veteran officers, who are men of experience [ĸ].
33 *I shall . . . tent* Q¹; not in F¹.   *presently* immediately.   36 *convenient* proper.
Pray go F¹; Q¹, ĸ: "Pray you go."   37 *I know the riddle* I understand her hidden
meaning; she is afraid to leave Edmund and me together [ĸ].   42 *For him* to
summon him.   44 *avouched* asserted.   *miscarry* are defeated in battle.   46 *And
. . . ceases* F¹; not in Q¹.   *machination* plotting (against your life).   50 *o'erlook*
read over.   51 *powers* troops.

Here is the guess of their true strength and forces
By diligent discovery; but your haste
Is now urg'd on you.

ALB.   We will greet the time.   *Exit.*

EDM.   To both these sisters have I sworn my love;   55
Each jealous of the other, as the stung
Are of the adder. Which of them shall I take?
Both? one? or neither? Neither can be enjoy'd,
If both remain alive. To take the widow
Exasperates, makes mad her sister Goneril;   60
And hardly shall I carry out my side,
Her husband being alive. Now then, we'll use
His countenance for the battle, which being done,
Let her who would be rid of him devise
His speedy taking off. As for the mercy   65
Which he intends to Lear and to Cordelia —
The battle done, and they within our power,
Shall never see his pardon; for my state
Stands on me to defend, not to debate.   *Exit.*

◇◇◇◇◇◇◇◇◇◇◇◇◇◇◇◇◇◇

SCENE II. [*A field between the two camps.*]

Alarum within. Enter, with Drum *and* Colours, *the*
Powers of France *over the stage,* Cordelia *with her*
Father *in her hand, and exeunt.*

Enter Edgar *and* Gloucester.

EDG.   Here, father, take the shadow of this tree
For your good host. Pray that the right may thrive.

---

53 *diligent discovery* careful reconnoitering.   53–4 *your haste . . . on you* rapid
action on your part is urgently necessary [K].   54 *greet the time* meet the demands
of the emergency promptly.   56 *jealous* suspicious.   61 *carry out my side* bring
my plans to a successful issue. Edmund aspires to the kingship [K].   63 *countenance* authority and support.   68–9 *my state . . . debate* the condition of my
affairs is such that it is incumbent on me to protect myself by action; it leaves me
no time to consider rights and wrongs [K].

> If ever I return to you again,
> I'll bring you comfort.

GLOU.   Grace go with you, sir!

Exit [Edgar].

Alarum and retreat within. Enter Edgar.

EDG.   Away, old man! give me thy hand! away!   5
King Lear hath lost, he and his daughter ta'en.
Give me thy hand! come on!

GLOU.   No further, sir. A man may rot even here.

EDG.   What, in ill thoughts again? Men must endure
Their going hence, even as their coming hither;   10
Ripeness is all. Come on.

GLOU.   And that's true too.   *Exeunt.*

◇◇◇◇◇◇◇◇◇◇◇◇◇◇◇◇

SCENE III. [*The British camp, near Dover.*]

Enter, in conquest, with Drum *and* Colours, Edmund;
Lear *and* Cordelia *as prisoners;* Soldiers, Captain.

EDM.   Some officers take them away. Good guard
Until their greater pleasures first be known
That are to censure them.

COR.   We are not the first
Who with best meaning have incurr'd the worst.
For thee, oppressed king, am I cast down;   5
Myself could else outfrown false Fortune's frown.

V.II. 2 *good host* shelterer.   4 *Grace* the favour of the gods [K].   9 *ill thoughts*
thoughts of suicide. *endure* suffer through.   10 *going hence* death. *coming*
hither birth.   11 *Ripeness is all* the only thing that is important in life is to be
ready for death when it comes [K].   *And . . . too* F¹; not in Q¹.

    V.III. 2 *their greater pleasures* the wishes of those persons of higher rank [K].
3 *censure* pass judgment on.   4 *meaning* intentions.

Shall we not see these daughters and these sisters?

LEAR. No, no, no, no! Come, let's away to prison.
We two alone will sing like birds i' th' cage.
When thou dost ask me blessing, I'll kneel down   10
And ask of thee forgiveness. So we'll live,
And pray, and sing, and tell old tales, and laugh
At gilded butterflies, and hear poor rogues
Talk of court news; and we'll talk with them too –
Who loses and who wins; who's in, who's out —   15
And take upon 's the mystery of things,
As if we were God's spies; and we'll wear out,
In a wall'd prison, packs and sects of great ones
That ebb and flow by th' moon.

EDM.   Take them away.

LEAR. Upon such sacrifices, my Cordelia,   20
The gods themselves throw incense. Have I caught thee?
He that parts us shall bring a brand from heaven
And fire us hence like foxes. Wipe thine eyes.
The goodyears shall devour 'em, flesh and fell,
Ere they shall make us weep! We'll see 'em starv'd first.   25
Come.

                    Exeunt [Lear *and* Cordelia, *guarded*].

EDM.   Come hither, Captain; hark.
Take thou this note [*gives a paper*]. Go follow them to
     prison.
One step I have advanc'd thee. If thou dost

---

13 *gilded butterflies* A common expression for gay, elaborately dressed courtiers.
16 *take upon's the mystery of things* assume (in our talk) that we can explain
all the mysteries of human affairs [K].   17 *As if we were God's spies* as if we
had been commissioned by God, as his angels, to survey the doings of mankind.
18 *packs* conniving cliques. *sects* parties, sets.   19 *ebb and flow by th' moon*
gain and lose by the month, as the moon changes.   20–1 *Upon such . . . incense* upon such sacrifices as thou has made for my sake the gods themselves attend
as priests [K].   22 *He . . . heaven* no human power shall ever part us again
[K].   23 *fire . . . foxes* as foxes are driven from their holes by fire and smoke [K].
24 *goodyears* evil forces, pestilence, or plague. The origin of the expression is uncertain, but it seems generally to have been used in this sense. *fell* skin.   27
this note This is Edmund's writ ordering the death of Lear and Cordelia. See lines
244–55. He has special authority as Regan's commissioned substitute in the cam-

As this instructs thee, thou dost make thy way
To noble fortunes. Know thou this, that men   30
Are as the time is. To be tender-minded
Does not become a sword. Thy great employment
Will not bear question. Either say thou'lt do't,
Or thrive by other means.

CAPT.   I'll do't, my lord.

EDM.   About it! and write happy when th' hast done.   35
Mark — I say, instantly; and carry it so
As I have set it down.

CAPT.   I cannot draw a cart, nor eat dried oats;
If it be man's work, I'll do't.   *Exit.*

            Flourish. Enter Albany, Goneril, Re-
            gan, Soldiers.

ALB.   Sir, you have show'd to-day your valiant strain,   40
And fortune led you well. You have the captives
Who were the opposites of this day's strife.
I do require them of you, so to use them
As we shall find their merits and our safety
May equally determine.

EDM.   Sir, I thought it fit   45
To send the old and miserable King
To some retention and appointed guard;
Whose age had charms in it, whose title more,
To pluck the common bosom on his side

---

paign (lines 63–4) [K].   30–1 *men . . . time is* i.e. they may be merciful in time of
peace but must be savage in war [K].   32 *become* befit.   33 *bear question* admit
discussion.   35 *write happy* call yourself fortunate.   36 *carry it so* manage the
affair in such a way.   38–9 *I cannot . . . I'll do't* A bit of rough humour based
on the proverbial contrast between a man and a horse (thought of as a stupid
animal and a beast of burden) [K] (Q¹; not in F¹).   40 *strain* lineage. Albany implies that Edmund has shown himself worthy of being a legitimate son of Gloucester [K].   42 *opposites* opponents, enemies.   43 *I do* F¹; Q¹, K: "We do."   44
merits desserts.   47 *To some . . . guard* to a place where they could be held in
custody by quards designated for that purpose [K].   48 *had* F¹; Q¹, K: "has."   49
To pluck . . . side to attract strongly the feelings of the rank and file of men to
take his part [K].

And turn our impress'd lances in our eyes   50
Which do command them. With him I sent the Queen,
My reason all the same; and they are ready
To-morrow, or at further space, t' appear
Where you shall hold your session. At this time
We sweat and bleed: the friend hath lost his friend;   55
And the best quarrels, in the heat, are curs'd
By those that feel their sharpness.
The question of Cordelia and her father
Requires a fitter place.

ALB.   Sir, by your patience,
I hold you but a subject of this war,   60
Not as a brother.

REG.   That's as we list to grace him.
Methinks our pleasure might have been demanded
Ere you had spoke so far. He led our powers,
Bore the commission of my place and person,
The which immediacy may well stand up   65
And call itself your brother.

GON.   Not so hot!
In his own grace he doth exalt himself
More than in your addition.

REG.   In my rights
By me invested, he compeers the best.

GON.   That were the most if he should husband you.   70

───

50 *impress'd* enlisted by conscription.   51 *Which* who.   54-9 *At this . . .
place* Q¹; not in F¹.   56 *quarrels* causes.   59 *Requires a fitter place* requires
for its settlement a fitter place than the camp [K]. *by your patience* if
you will not be offended by my frankness. A phrase of courteous apology [K].
61 *list* choose. *grace* honour.   62 *pleasure* wishes. *demanded* asked.   64 *Bore
. . . and person* had the authority belonging to my rank and represented me personally [K].   65 *The which immediacy* and the fact that he was thus my immediate representative, clothed with all my authority [K].   67 *grace* merit and
honour.   68 *addition* titles bestowed upon him.   69 *compeers* equals.   70 *were
the most* would be the fullest (investiture in your rights).   72 *look'd but asquint*
did not see straight.   74 *full-flowing stomach* a full tide of angry resentment.
"Stomach" for "wrath" is common [K].   76 *Dispose . . . thine* F¹; not in Q¹.
are F², F¹: "is." *walls are thine* you have won the walls; you have taken my de-

REG.   Jesters do oft prove prophets.

GON.   Holla, holla!
       That eye that told you so look'd but asquint.

REG.   Lady, I am not well; else I should answer
       From a full-flowing stomach. General,
       Take thou my soldiers, prisoners, patrimony;   75
       Dispose of them, of me; the walls are thine.
       Witness the world that I create thee here
       My lord and master.

GON.   Mean you to enjoy him?

ALB.   The let-alone lies not in your good will.

EDM.   Nor in thine, lord.

ALB.   Half-blooded fellow, yes.   80

REG.   [*to* Edmund] Let the drum strike, and prove my title
           thine.

ALB.   Stay yet; hear reason. Edmund, I arrest thee
       On capital treason; and, in thine attaint,
       This gilded serpent [*points to* Goneril]. For your claim,
           fair sister,
       I bar it in the interest of my wife.   85
       'Tis she is subcontracted to this lord,
       And I, her husband, contradict your banes.
       If you will marry, make your loves to me;
       My lady is bespoke.

GON.   An interlude!

---

fences by storm. The metaphor by which a woman or a woman's heart is identified with a castle or walled town defending itself against besiegers was common
in the Middle Ages and had become conventional long before Shakespeare's time
[K].   78 *enjoy* possess.   79 *let-alone* prohibition.   80 *Half-blooded fellow*
bastard.   83 *in thine attaint* as a sharer in the treason of which you are guilty.
Treason was a crime that "corrupted the blood" of the traitor — i.e. deprived his
kindred of their civil rights [K] (Q¹; F¹: "in thy arrest").   85 *bar* ROWE; F¹, Q¹:
"bare."   86 *subcontracted* bound by a contract which depends for its validity on
the fulfillment or abrogation of a previous contract [K]. Albany, of course, is being
sarcastic.   87 *banes* banns, announcements of intention to marry.   88 *loves*
courtship.   89 *bespoke* betrothed. *interlude* farce. An "interlude" was a brief
play, usually comical — so called from its coming in an interval of festivities.
Goneril's contempt for her husband's irony seems well deserved [K].

ALB.	Thou art arm'd, Gloucester. Let the trumpet sound.	90

ALB.   Thou art arm'd, Gloucester. Let the trumpet sound.   90
If none appear to prove upon thy person
Thy heinous, manifest, and many treasons,
There is my pledge [*throws down a glove*]! I'll make it
    on thy heart,
Ere I taste bread, thou art in nothing less
Than I have here proclaim'd thee.

REG.   Sick, O, sick!   95

GON.   [*aside*] If not, I'll ne'er trust medicine.

EDM.   There's my exchange [*throws down a glove*]. What in
    the world he is
That names me traitor, villain-like he lies.
Call by thy trumpet. He that dares approach,
On him, on you, who not? I will maintain   100
My truth and honour firmly.

ALB.   A herald, ho!

EDM.   A herald, ho, a herald!

ALB.   Trust to thy single virtue; for thy soldiers,
All levied in my name, have in my name
Took their discharge.

REG.   My sickness grows upon me.   105

ALB.   She is not well. Convey her to my tent.

                       [*Exit* Regan, *led.*]

           Enter a Herald.

Come hither, herald. Let the trumpet sound,
And read out this.

CAPT.   Sound, trumpet!   *A trumpet sounds.*

---

90 *Thou art arm'd* Edmund still wears the armour he wore in the battle [K]. *Let
. . . sound* Albany is acting in accordance with the instructions that he has received from Edgar in the letter mentioned in V.I. 40 [K].   93 *make it* demonstrate
it to be true (F¹; Q¹, K: "proue it").   94 *in nothing* in no one detail.   96 *medicine*
Goneril has poisoned her sister [K].   97 *What* whoever and of whatever rank.
102 *A herald, ho, a herald* Q¹; not in F¹.   103 *single virtue* unaided ability.   105
grows upon begins to overpower.   109 *Sound, trumpet* Q¹; not in F¹.   110 *quality
or degree* rank or high position.   111 *lists* limits.   122 *canker-bit* eaten away by

HER.	(*reads*) "If any man of quality or degree within the lists 110 of the army will maintain upon Edmund, supposed Earl of Gloucester, that he is a manifold traitor, let him appear by the third sound of the trumpet. He is bold in his defence."
EDM.	Sound! *First trumpet.* 115
HER.	Again! *Second trumpet.*
HER.	Again! *Third trumpet.*

Trumpet answers within.

Enter Edgar, *armed, at the third sound, a* Trumpet *before him.*

ALB.	Ask him his purposes, why he appears Upon this call o' th' trumpet.
HER.	What are you? Your name, your quality? and why you answer 120 This present summons?
EDG.	Know my name is lost; By treason's tooth bare-gnawn and canker-bit. Yet am I noble as the adversary I come to cope.
ALB.	Which is that adversary?
EDG.	What's he that speaks for Edmund Earl of Gloucester? 125
EDM.	Himself. What say'st thou to him?
EDG.	Draw thy sword, That, if my speech offend a noble heart, Thy arm may do thee justice. Here is mine. Behold, it is the privilege of mine honours,

the canker — a caterpillar that feeds on rosebuds, destroying them before they open. 124 *cope* cope with, meet in combat.   128 *arm* sword.   129 *the privilege of mine honours* Edgar means that, being a knight, he has the privilege of his knighthood — namely, to challenge to single combat anyone whom he has reason to accuse of an offence against knightly honour. Treason is the most flagrant of such offences [K] (POPE; F¹: "my priuiledge, The priuiledge of mine Honours"; Q¹: "the priuiledge of my tongue") .

My oath, and my profession. I protest —   130
Maugre thy strength, youth, place, and eminence,
Despite thy victor sword and fire-new fortune,
Thy valour and thy heart — thou art a traitor;
False to thy gods, thy brother, and thy father;
Conspirant 'gainst this high illustrious prince;   135
And from th' extremest upward of thy head
To the descent and dust below thy foot,
A most toad-spotted traitor. Say thou "no,"
This sword, this arm, and my best spirits are bent
To prove upon thy heart, whereto I speak,   140
Thou liest.

EDM.   In wisdom I should ask thy name;
But since thy outside looks so fair and warlike,
And that thy tongue some say of breeding breathes,
What safe and nicely I might well delay
By rule of knighthood, I disdain and spurn.   145
Back do I toss those treasons to thy head;
With the hell-hated lie o'erwhelm thy heart;
Which — for they yet glance by and scarcely bruise —
This sword of mine shall give them instant way
Where they shall rest for ever. Trumpets, speak!   150

Alarums. Fight. [Edmund *falls.*]

ALB.   Save him, save him!

GON.   This is practice, Gloucester.
By th' law of arms thou wast not bound to answer
An unknown opposite. Thou art not vanquish'd,

---

130 *My oath* the oath I swore when I was dubbed knight [K].   *profession*
function — as knight.   131 *Maugre* in spite of.   132 *victor* victorious (in the
recent battle).   *fire-new* brand-new — just finished on the smith's forge. Edgar
refers to Edmund's recent elevation to the rank of Earl of Gloucester [K].   133
heart courage.   135 *Conspirant* engaged in a conspiracy.   137 *To the descent . . .
foot* to the sole of thy foot and the dust beneath it [K].   *below* F¹; Q¹, K: "beneath."
138 *toad-spotted* spotted with treason as the toad is marked with spots that exude
venom [K].   139 *bent* directed.   140 *whereto I speak* Edgar's accusation comes
from the heart and is addressed to the heart and conscience of Edmund [K].   141
wisdom prudence. He is not bound by his knighthood to fight with a man of
lower social rank.   143 *some say of breeding breathes* shows some touch (say) of
a gentleman's education [K].   144 *What safe . . . delay* F¹; not in Q¹.   144-5 *What*

But cozen'd and beguil'd.

ALB.   Shut your mouth, dame,
Or with this paper shall I stop it. [*Shows her her letter
  to* Edmund.] — [*To* Edmund]. Hold, sir.   155
[*To* Goneril] Thou worse than any name, read thine
  own evil.
No tearing, lady! I perceive you know it.

GON.   Say if I do — the laws are mine, not thine.
Who can arraign me for't?

ALB.   Most monstrous! O!
Know'st thou this paper?

GON.   Ask me not what I know.   160

                                                    Exit.

ALB.   Go after her. She's desperate; govern her.

                                        [*Exit an* Officer.]

EDM.   What you have charg'd me with, that have I done,
And more, much more. The time will bring it out.
'Tis past, and so am I. — But what art thou
That hast this fortune on me? If thou'rt noble,   165
I do forgive thee.

EDG.   Let's exchange charity.
I am no less in blood than thou art, Edmund;
If more, the more th' hast wrong'd me.
My name is Edgar and thy father's son.
The gods are just, and of our pleasant vices   170
Make instruments to plague us.

---

safe . . . spurn I scorn to delay the combat, as I might delay it, in accordance
with the code of chivalry, if I cared to insist on the strict rules of the code [K].
safe without infringing upon the rules. *nicely* punctiliously.   147 *hell-hated* hateful as hell.   148 *Which* i.e. the treasons.   150 *Where . . . ever* if he succeeds in
the battle the treason will remain forever with the defeated Edgar.   151 *Save
him* Apparently Albany does not wish Edmund to die until he has had a chance
to expose him by means of the letter.   151 *practice* trickery (F¹; Q¹, K: "mere practice").   152 *arms* Q¹; F¹: "Warre."   154 *cozen'd* cheated.   159 *O* F¹; not in Q¹, K.
161 *govern* restrain.   166 *exchange charity* forgive one another.   168 *If more* if
greater (since he is legitimate and Edmund is not).   171 *plague* F¹; Q¹, K·
"scourge."

The dark and vicious place where thee he got
Cost him his eyes.

EDM. 　　　　　　　　Th' hast spoken right; 'tis true.
The wheel is come full circle; I am here.

ALB. 　　Methought thy very gait did prophesy　　　　175
A royal nobleness. I must embrace thee.
Let sorrow split my heart if ever I
Did hate thee, or thy father!

EDG. 　　　　　　　　　'　Worthy prince, I know't.

ALB. 　　Where have you hid yourself?
How have you known the miseries of your father?　　180

EDG. 　　By nursing them, my lord. List a brief tale;
And when 'tis told, O that my heart would burst!
The bloody proclamation to escape
That follow'd me so near (O, our lives' sweetness!
That we the pain of death would hourly die　　　　185
Rather than die at once!) taught me to shift
Into a madman's rags, t' assume a semblance
That very dogs disdain'd; and in this habit
Met I my father with his bleeding rings,
Their precious stones new lost; became his guide,　　190
Led him, begg'd for him, sav'd him from despair;
Never (O fault!) reveal'd myself unto him
Until some half hour past, when I was arm'd,
Not sure, though hoping of this good success,
I ask'd his blessing, and from first to last　　　　195
Told him our pilgrimage. But his flaw'd heart
(Alack, too weak the conflict to support!)

---

172 *place* the adulterous bed. *got* begot. 174 *The wheel . . . here* I began life
at the very lowest point on Fortune's wheel. As the wheel revolved, I rose to the
summit. Now its revolution is completed, and here I am — at the very bottom,
where I was at the beginning. Fortune sits by her wheel and turns it constantly
(cf. II.II.168). On this wheel are mortals, who are therefore sometimes rising,
sometimes at the summit, and sometimes descending or at the very bottom of
their fate [K]. 175 *prophesy* promise. 181 *List* listen to. 185-6 *That we . . .
at once* that we prefer to continually suffer the pain of death rather than die at
once. *That we* F¹; Q¹, K: "That with." 189 *rings* eye sockets. 192 *fault* error in

'Twixt two extremes of passion, joy and grief,
Burst smilingly.

EDM.   This speech of yours hath mov'd me,
And shall perchance do good; but speak you on;   200
You look as you had something more to say.

ALB.   If there be more, more woeful, hold it in;
For I am almost ready to dissolve,
Hearing of this.

EDG.   This would have seem'd a period
To such as love not sorrow; but another,   205
To amplify too much, would make much more,
And top extremity.
Whilst I was big in clamour, came there a man,
Who, having seen me in my worst estate,
Shunn'd my abhorr'd society; but then, finding   210
Who 'twas that so endur'd, with his strong arms
He fastened on my neck, and bellowed out
As he'd burst heaven; threw him on my father;
Told the most piteous tale of Lear and him
That ever ear receiv'd; which in recounting   215
His grief grew puissant, and the strings of life
Began to crack. Twice then the trumpets sounded,
And there I left him tranc'd.

ALB.   But who was this?

EDG.   Kent, sir, the banish'd Kent; who in disguise
Followed his enemy king and did him service   220
Improper for a slave.

                   Enter a Gentleman *with a bloody
                   knife.*

---

judgment.   196 *our* F¹; Q¹, к: "my."   *pilgrimage* journey, wanderings about together.   *flaw'd* i.e. on account of what it had already suffered [к].   203 *dissolve*
melt into tears.   204–21 *This would . . . a slave* Q¹; not in F¹.   204 *This would
. . . period* it would have seemed that sorrow had run its course [к].   208 *big in
clamour* loud in my lamentations [к].   209 *estate* condition.   213 *threw him on
my father* threw himself on the body of my father [к].   *him on* THEOBALD; Q¹:
"me on."   216 *puissant* powerful, overmastering.   *strings of life* heartstrings.
221 *Improper for a slave* unfitting even for a slave [к].

GENT.	Help, help! O, help!
EDG.	What kind of help?
ALB.	Speak, man.
EDG.	What means that bloody knife?
GENT.	'Tis hot, it smokes.
	It came even from the heart of — O, she's dead!
ALB.	Who dead? Speak, man. 225
GENT.	Your lady, sir, your lady! and her sister
	By her is poisoned; she hath confess'd it.
EDM.	I was contracted to them both. All three
	Now marry in an instant.

Enter Kent.

EDG.	Here comes Kent.
ALB.	Produce the bodies, be they alive or dead. 230

[*Exit* Gentleman.]

This judgment of the heavens, that makes us tremble,
Touches us not with pity. O, is this he?
The time will not allow the compliment
That very manners urges.

KENT.	I am come
	To bid my king and master aye good night. 235
	Is he not here?
ALB.	Great thing of us forgot!
	Speak, Edmund, where's the King? and where's Cordelia?

The bodies of Goneril *and* Regan *are
brought in.*

Seest thou this object, Kent?

---

223 *smokes* steams.   229 *marry* are united (by death).   230 *the* F[1]; Q[1], K: "their."
233 *compliment* ceremony.   235 *aye* for ever.   236 *Great thing . . . forgot* This
amnesia on everybody's part is necessary for the climax that follows, but — though
the audience thinks little of it — the reader always feels a shock [K].   238 *this
object* this sight. In Elizabethan English "object" often means all that one sees at

KENT.   Alack, why thus?

EDM.   Yet Edmund was belov'd.
        The one the other poisoned for my sake,   240
        And after slew herself.

ALB.   Even so. Cover their faces.

EDM.   I pant for life. Some good I mean to do,
        Despite of mine own nature. Quickly send
        (Be brief in't) to the castle; for my writ   245
        Is on the life of Lear and on Cordelia.
        Nay, send in time.

ALB.   Run, run, O, run!

EDG.   To who, my lord? Who has the office? Send
        Thy token of reprieve.

EDM.   Well thought on. Take my sword;   250
        Give it the Captain.

ALB.   Haste thee for thy life.

                                        [*Exit* Edgar.]

EDM.   He hath commission from thy wife and me
        To hang Cordelia in the prison and
        To lay the blame upon her own despair
        That she fordid herself.   255

ALB.   The gods defend her! Bear him hence awhile.

                            [Edmund *is borne off.*]

                Enter Lear, *with* Cordelia [*dead*] *in
                his arms,* [Edgar, Captain, *and others
                following*].

LEAR.   Howl, howl, howl! O, you are men of stones.
        Had I your tongues and eyes, I'ld use them so
        That heaven's vault should crack. She's gone for ever!

---

the moment [K].   239 *Yet* after all, in spite of everything.   241 *after* afterwards.
248 *office* commission.   250 *my sword* as proof that you are the bearer of orders
from me [K].   251 *Haste . . . life* Q¹; F¹ gives the speech to Edgar.   255 *fordid
herself* committed suicide.   257 *Howl . . . howl* F¹; the word is repeated four
times in Q¹, K.   *stones* F¹, Q¹; POPE, K: "stone."

I know when one is dead, and when one lives.   260
She's dead as earth. Lend me a looking glass.
If that her breath will mist or stain the stone,
Why, then she lives.

KENT.   Is this the promis'd end?

EDG.   Or image of that horror?

ALB.   Fall and cease!

LEAR.   This feather stirs; she lives! If it be so,   265
It is a chance which does redeem all sorrows
That ever I have felt.

KENT.   O my good master!

LEAR.   Prithee away!

EDG.   'Tis noble Kent, your friend.

LEAR.   A plague upon you, murderers, traitors all!
I might have sav'd her; now she's gone for ever!   270
Cordelia, Cordelia! stay a little. Ha!
What is't thou say'st? Her voice was ever soft,
Gentle, and low — an excellent thing in woman.
I kill'd the slave that was a-hanging thee.

CAPT.   'Tis true, my lords, he did.

LEAR.   Did I not, fellow?   275
I have seen the day, with my good biting falchion
I would have made them skip. I am old now,
And these same crosses spoil me. Who are you?
Mine eyes are not o' th' best. I'll tell you straight.

---

262 *stone* surface of the mirror.   263 *the promis'd end* the Day of Doom that
the prophets foretell [K].   264 *image* exact likeness. *Fall and Cease* Addressed
to the universe: "Let the end of all things come [K].   266 *redeem* repay in full;
atone for [K].   270 *I might have sav'd her* We are not to suppose that Cordelia
was alive when Lear brought her in. He was deluded by his desperate hope [K].
276 *falchion* a small light sword with the point bent inward.   277 *them* Q¹; F¹:
"him."   278 *these same crosses* these troubles of mine. A "cross" is anything that
vexes or thwarts one [K].   279 *straight* in a moment.   280-1 *If fortune . . .
behold* in the whole course of human history we cannot find a stranger example
of Fortune's inconstancy than Lear's life affords [K].   282 *dull sight* Either

KENT. If fortune brag of two she lov'd and hated,   280
        One of them we behold.

LEAR. This' a dull sight. Are you not Kent?

KENT.   The same —
        Your servant Kent. Where is your servant Caius?

LEAR. He's a good fellow, I can tell you that.
        He'll strike, and quickly too. He's dead and rotten.   285

KENT. No, my good lord; I am the very man —

LEAR. I'll see that straight.

KENT. That from your first of difference and decay
        Have followed your sad steps.

LEAR.   You're welcome hither.

KENT. Nor no man else! All's cheerless, dark, and deadly.   290
        Your eldest daughters have fordone themselves,
        And desperately are dead.

LEAR.   Ay, so I think.

ALB.   He knows not what he says; and vain is it
        That we present us to him.

EDG.   Very bootless.

                    Enter a Captain.

CAPT. Edmund is dead, my lord.

ALB.   That's but a trifle here.   295
        You lords and noble friends, know our intent.
        What comfort to this great decay may come

(a) melancholy spectacle, the body of Cordelia, or (b) his own failing eyesight.
Critics have been divided.   283 *Caius* the name Kent had assumed in disguise.
287 *see* attend to. *straight* immediately.   288 *from your . . . decay* from the very
beginning of your decline in fortunes. "Decay is synonymous with "difference" [K].
290 *Nor no man else* nor is any one else welcome. Kent implies that this is a time
when no one can be greeted as a guest — this is no occasion for the courtesies of
normal life [K].   291 *foredone* destroyed.   292 *desperately* in despair.   294 *bootless* useless, in vain.   297 *comfort* help and support. *this great decay* this great
man, thus fallen into weakness. Such use of an abstract noun to describe a person
was common in Elizabethan English [K].

> Shall be applied. For us, we will resign,
> During the life of this old Majesty,
> To him our absolute power; [*to* Edgar *and* Kent] you to
>   your rights;   300
> With boot, and such addition as your honours
> Have more than merited. — All friends shall taste
> The wages of their virtue, and all foes
> The cup of their deservings. — O, see, see!

LEAR.   And my poor fool is hang'd! No, no, no life!   305
    Why should a dog, a horse, a rat, have life,
    And thou no breath at all? Thou'lt come no more,
    Never, never, never, never, never!
    Pray you undo this button. Thank you, sir.
    Do you see this? Look on her! look! her lips!   310
    Look there, look there!   *He dies.*

EDG.   He faints! My lord, my lord!

KENT.   Break, heart; I prithee break!

EDG.   Look up, my lord.

KENT.   Vex not his ghost. O, let him pass! He hates him
    That would upon the rack of this tough world
    Stretch him out longer.

EDG.   He is gone indeed.   315

KENT.   The wonder is, he hath endur'd so long.
    He but usurp'd his life.

ALB.   Bear them from hence. Our present business

---

298 *resign* The play ends as it had begun, with a resignation of kingship; Lear dies restored to the kingship he had surrendered.   301 *boot* addition.   302 *taste* experience.   305 *my poor fool* i.e. Cordelia. "Fool" was often used as a term of affection [K]. If, as has been suggested, Cordelia and The Fool were played by the same boy actor, both characters may be here indicated. Some critics have held that Lear, his mind wandering, is no longer capable of distinguishing between the two people he has most fully loved.   309 *this button* The button is at Lear's throat — for he feels suffocation — not one of Cordelia's buttons, as has been sometimes suggested.   310-11 *Do you . . . there* F¹; not in Q¹.   311 *look there* It has been suggested by some critics — most notably A. C. Bradley and R. W. Chambers — that Lear dies in a final burst of joy, thinking that Cordelia lives. If

Is general woe. [*To* Kent *and* Edgar] Friends of my soul,
    you twain
Rule in this realm, and the gor'd state sustain.   320

KENT.   I have a journey, sir, shortly to go.
         My master calls me; I must not say no.

ALB.   The weight of this sad time we must obey,
         Speak what we feel, not what we ought to say.
         The oldest hath borne most; we that are young   325
         Shall never see so much, nor live so long.

                        Exeunt with a dead march.

---

so, his death would parallel closely that of Gloucester, both being influenced by Sidney's account in THE ARCADIA of the death of the blind King of Paphlagonia. The matter has been one of great critical controversy.   313 *his ghost* his departing spirit [K].   314 *the rack* A common torture in Shakespeare's time. The victim was extended and bound upon a frame and levers were applied to stretch his joints even to dislocation [K].   317 *usurp'd* possessed wrongfully — he has lived longer than any man naturally should.   323-6 *The weight . . . so long* Q¹; F¹ gives the speech to Edgar. The Quartos are correct, for such a concluding speech (serving as an epilogue) would, in a tragedy, regularly be assigned to the person of highest rank who survives [K].   325 *hath* F¹; Q¹, K: "haue."